THE PATH OF TRANSFOR· MATION

NATARAJ
PUBLISHING

MILL VALLEY, CALIFORNIA

SHAKTI GAWAIN

THE PATH OF TRANSFOR· MATION

How Healing Ourselves Can Change The World

THE PATH OF TRANSFORMATION
How Healing Ourselves Can Change the World

© 1993 Shakti Gawain

Published by Nataraj Publishing
P.O. Box 2430
Mill Valley, CA 94942

Edited by Hal Zina Bennett
Cover art and design by Greg Wittrock
Cover photo by Irene Young
Cover photo hand colored by Loretta Paul
Typography by TBH/Typecast, Inc.

The author of this book does not dispense medical advice or prescribe the use of any technique as a form of treatment for physical or mental problems without the advice of a physician, either directly or indirectly. In the event you use any of the information in this book, neither the author nor the publisher can assume any responsibility for your actions. The intent of the author is only to offer information of a general nature to help you in your quest for personal growth.

Library of Congress Cataloging-in-Publication Data

Gawain, Shakti, 1948-
Path of transformation : how healing ourselves can change the
    world / by Shakti Gawain.
p.   cm.
ISBN 1-882591-15-1 : $11.95
1. Conduct of life.   I. Title.
BJ1581.G   1993
158'.1—dc20
                                        93-10940
                                        CIP

00 99 98 97   9 8 7 6
First printing, November 1993
Sixth printing, May 1997

Printed in the USA

To all the teachers and friends who have helped
me along my own transformational path.

ACKNOWLEDGEMENTS

My heartfelt thanks go to my editor, Hal Bennett. Your creativity and expertise have added greatly to the book, and to my enjoyment in writing it.

I'd like to express my appreciation to Jane Hogan for your vision and hard work in the creation of Nataraj Publishing, Kathy Altman for the ideas you contributed to the book and your overall support, Karen Lamoreux for your work in shaping the book, and all the other people associated with Nataraj Publishing who have helped, directly or indirectly, to bring this book into form.

Last, but certainly not least, a special thanks to my husband and partner, Jim Burns, for your loving support on all levels.

CONTENTS

ONE

HOW WE CAN
CHANGE THE WORLD

TWO

ON THE PATH
OF TRANSFORMATION

WHO THIS BOOK IS FOR

If you have just picked up this book and are wondering whether or not you want to read it, perhaps the following will help you out. If one or more of the following statements applies to you, then the chances are very good that you will find this book worthwhile reading:

◆ You are facing one or more major challenges in your personal life regarding your health and well-being, your relationships, your life work, your finances, creativity, or anything else.

◆ You are deeply concerned about world problems such as famine, disease, poverty, war, racism, sexism, drug addiction, the disintegration of the family, the destruction of the environment, and you are:

Doing everything in your power to find solutions to these problems on social, political and/or spiritual levels; or,

Feeling helpless, not knowing what to do about these seemingly overwhelming problems, wondering what, if anything, you can do to really make a difference;

◆ You have been on a consciousness journey for some time, doing a lot of inner work. You're feeling ready to move back out into the world, but you're not quite sure how to make the transition from inner to outer work with integrity. And perhaps you're wondering how relevant all your consciousness work is in terms of finding solutions to the tough global problems of today.

◆ You have done a lot of spiritual practice, perhaps devoted to one or more specific paths or teachers, yet you are feeling stuck in certain areas of your life. You are wondering why you aren't progressing faster, or why you can't apply your spiritual knowledge more successfully in your daily life.

◆ You have done a lot of psychological work on yourself and are yearning for a more expanded vision of life's possibilities.

◆ You have done a lot of work in recovery (healing an addiction or dependency) and are wondering what's next.

◆ You are a "New Age" person who holds an optimistic view of life, but wonder why you keep encountering painful experiences or angry, needy, or otherwise "unenlightened" people.

◆ You are drawn toward doing consciousness work, but you can't stand the "flakier" aspects of the New Age movement.

◆ You have never done any consciousness work that you know of, and you aren't even sure what it is, but you sense the need for something deeper and more meaningful in your life.

◆ You are going through a major transition in your life, letting go of something old and opening to the new.

◆ You've been experiencing upset or upheaval in your life, and you are wondering why.

Well, the list turned out to be a bit longer than I expected. But there you are. Try on the different "shoes" I describe, and if any of them fit, put them on and keep walking up the path . . .

WHY I WROTE
THIS BOOK

As we rapidly approach the new millennium, life on our planet seems to be intensifying. Most of us are faced with challenging personal problems — in our jobs, our relationships and families, our finances, our health. We're not sure how to best meet these challenges. Our traditional ways of living, working and relating to each other and our environment don't seem to be functioning very well anymore, yet we have few role models for effective new ways.

Even more overwhelming are the problems confronting humanity as a whole. On a planetary level, things seem to be getting worse and worse. We wonder why there is so much pain, suffering, and struggle all over the world. Most of us have no idea of what we can do to help, so we do little or nothing.

I wrote this book to address these issues and to share the ideas and perspectives that have helped me the most in facing my own problems and the global situation. I want to clarify the challenges I see facing us in the '90s and how we can best meet them. My intentions are to provide understanding and tools for dealing more effectively with personal issues, and to explain from my own viewpoint why the world is in such turmoil and what I believe we can do about it.

I also wish to address some of the confusion I see in the consciousness movement, otherwise known as the New Age

movement, or human potential movement. As I have trav-
eled around for many years, giving workshops all over the
world, I have grown concerned about certain issues that
many sincere seekers seem to be struggling with. I believe
that a number of these struggles arise from the fact that
many New Age philosophies and leaders are drawing from
wisdom of ancient spiritual traditions without fully adapt-
ing them to the modern world and our present stage of
human evolution. Too many people are striving to follow a
path which, as I see it, ultimately will not meet their needs
or the needs of the world.

Another issue I have tried to address here is that many
traditional forms of psychotherapy, while providing a certain amount of help and guidance, exclude the spiritual or
transpersonal dimension of human life, and so leave out a
significant part of the healing paradigm. Since a majority of
people in the modern world are suffering from a lack of any
connection with their spiritual essence, this leaves a major
hole in the healing process. All too often, the deeper levels of
emotional healing are not dealt with, either. Few clients or
therapists know where to turn for profound healing on all
levels.

I am concerned, as well, by the growing chasm I see
between many people who are conscientiously working to
effect political, social, and environmental reform, and those
who are equally committed to their consciousness growth
process. Both groups have visions of a healthier, more harmonious world and a commitment to work hard for positive
change. However, there is little agreement about how real
change can be accomplished. We need to work together, to
understand and respect each others' contributions.

Changing our lives and changing the world cannot be
accomplished either by focusing exclusively on external
solutions or by following a traditional transcendent, spiritual path in which the reality and importance of the physical world is minimized or denied. Rather, we need to choose

an alternative which I call the path of transformation, in which we commit ourselves to the integration of our spiritual and human aspects and learn to live as whole beings, in balance and fulfillment on the earth.

Today's challenges can only be met powerfully and effectively through a shift in consciousness, which in fact is already well under way worldwide. We need to recognize, to the depths of our souls, that we are all part of one whole, that what each of us does individually has a powerful impact on us all. Our global crises relate to and mirror our individual processes. Only through healing ourselves on all levels—physical, emotional, mental and spiritual—can we heal the planet.

I hope this book can provide guidance for readers at all stages of the consciousness journey—those who are just beginning as well as those who are already on the path and wish to move deeper. It is my wish that what I've written here will help all my readers grasp the importance of healing, developing and integrating all aspects of our being.

I hope, also, that what I've tried to communicate in these pages will be helpful to those who have done considerable inner work and integration on all levels already and now want to bring their knowledge forth into the world in meaningful and powerful ways.

The message of this book is really quite simple: Each one of us makes a real and substantial difference on this planet. And by making a commitment to your own consciousness journey, you are indeed taking a significant role in the transformation of the world.

ONE

How We Can Change the World

Never doubt that a small group of thoughtful, committed citizens can change the world. Indeed it is the only thing that ever has.

—Margaret Mead

WHAT IS YOUR VISION
OF THE FUTURE?

In this book we will be exploring our thoughts, feelings, fears, and visions about our own personal futures, and the future of our world. Before you read further, I'd like to invite you to do the brief exercise that follows. The purpose of this exercise is to help you get in touch with some of your own thoughts and feelings before reading what I have to say.

So before you start reading the first chapter, I'd like to ask you to take a few moments, read through the following exercise once, then close your eyes and try it. (If you prefer not to do this, that's fine—just go on to the first chapter.)

Sit comfortably in a quiet place. If you wish, have a pen and paper or your journal within easy reach. Close your eyes and take a few slow, deep breaths. Ask yourself, "What is my vision of the future? How do I feel about it?"

First, focus your attention on how you see, think and feel about your own personal future. How do you imagine your future prospects in your career, your finances, your relationships, your family, friends, your physical health and fitness (including how you feel about your aging process), and your overall personal wellbeing?

Just sit quietly and note whatever thoughts, feelings and images come up for you. Try to be very honest with yourself and acknowledge all the thoughts and feelings you have about these things, both positive and negative. Some of your inner responses to these questions might seem contradictory or confusing. For example, you might simultaneously have both positive and negative feelings about the same thing. That's perfectly natural and quite okay. Just acknowledge the full range of your feelings.

Now, expand your focus to imagine the future of your community, your country, humanity, the natural environment, the planet. Just notice the images, thoughts and feelings that come to you when you ask yourself to imagine the future of the world. Again, try to be as honest as you can and don't worry if your inner responses seem somewhat contradictory or confusing. For example, you might find yourself thinking, "There's so much potential for positive changes . . . but I wonder if we will destroy ourselves before we get a chance to make those changes!"

When you feel complete with the exercise, open your eyes. If you wish, take your pen and paper or your journal and write down as much as you can about what came to you as you imagined your personal future and the future of our planet. If you prefer, use colored pens or crayons and draw your images and feelings.

Facing the Future

Humanity is in an ongoing process of conscious evolution. At this time, we are taking a giant step in consciousness—a great leap in that evolutionary process.

How do you feel about the future? If you are like most of us, you may find yourself having very mixed feelings when you consider that question.

If you are an especially optimistic person, or happen to be having a particularly good day, you might imagine a bright, glowing future for yourself and for all of us. If you're a more cynical or pessimistic person, or if you are having a difficult day, you may may foresee a dim or dark future for yourself and others.

I've found, however, that most people who are asked this question, myself included, experience at least some conflicting feelings. On one hand we feel hope, excitement, a certain fascination with what the future may bring. On the other hand, we feel some doubt, fear, perhaps even dread or despair. Oftentimes we feel a deep confusion and helplessness about what to do. We barely know how to effectively address our own personal problems, much less the gigantic problems we see out there in the world.

It is entirely appropriate that so many of us are experiencing this mixture of feelings. Nobody would deny that this is a very scary time, perhaps the most frightening time that has ever existed on this planet. Most people are struggling with painful personal problems. Our relationships don't seem to be working the way we think they should. Marriages are falling apart. Children are being abused. Many people are addicted to drugs. A friend, family member (or we ourselves) may be suffering from a disease for which we have no cure. Some of us have no jobs; others are dissatisfied with the jobs we have. Many of us are workaholics who are burning ourselves out. Perhaps we are dealing with our own or a loved one's addictions to alcohol, drugs, food, or other substances or activities.

As if all this weren't enough, when we look beyond our personal lives, we see even worse problems. We have wars all over the planet. Many countries are suffering from cruel, repressive governments. The Third World countries are being exploited by the industrialized nations. Economic chaos and disasters are threatening. We have increasing violence in our cities, and homelessness has become a terrible problem. We have a drug epidemic that's out of control. Probably most frightening of all, we are in the process of destroying the natural environment upon which our lives depend.

It's unpleasant and uncomfortable to face these realities and our feelings about them, so most of us try to focus on other things. Yet, in order to have the courage to confront our personal and planetary problems, and try to solve them, we must first be honest enough to acknowledge the confusing, frightening feelings we may have and how overwhelming it all seems. The first step we must take in dealing with any challenge is to acknowledge what it is and how we feel about it. It is only through facing our fears and difficulties that we can find creative and effective solutions.

If our personal lives are so difficult, and the world is in such a mess (reconfirmed every evening on the news) why should we feel anything except despair? Why feel hopeful at all? The reason is that although this is a frightening time, it is simultaneously the most powerful time that has ever existed on this planet.

Humanity is in an ongoing process of conscious evolution. At this time, we are taking a giant step in consciousness—a great leap in that evolutionary process. It's probably the most exciting event that has ever taken place on this plane of reality. And I believe that on a soul level we have all chosen to be here at this time in order to take part in it. So we've committed ourselves to being here and doing this, we've put our hearts and souls into it, and now we're looking rather anxiously and breathlessly to see whether or not it's going to work! Somewhere, deep inside us, we know what is possible, and we're wondering if we're going to be able to manifest that. It's a big question.

I believe that the answer to that question lies in the hands of every one of us. Through our personal commitment to the process of growth and change, each of us has the power not only to transform our own life, but to contribute tremendously to the transformation of life on our planet.

Healing Crises
in Our Personal Lives

---

*A healing crisis occurs at the point where we
have outgrown an old pattern or way of being,
but are still unconsciously holding onto that old
way because it feels safe and familiar.*

As you may have noticed, it often takes a personal crisis of some kind to catalyze real change and growth in our lives. Upon reflection, you can probably remember how a period of great upheaval, filled with confusion and pain, perhaps triggered by an event such as the death of a loved one, the ending of a relationship, a financial setback or loss of a job, or an accident or illness, has ultimately led to greater understanding, awareness and new opportunities in your life. If you look at the lives of people you know, you may very well see the same pattern. Times of chaos and uncertainty can lead to new doors opening, especially when we are willing and able to look for the growth opportunities in a situation rather than simply being overwhelmed by outside circumstances.

It is the nature of the human soul to constantly move forward into greater challenge, expansion, and awareness. The primary job of the human personality, however, is to try to survive in physical form and get our physical and emotional

needs met as best we can. There are certain parts of our personalities that want to change and grow, recognizing that
growing is necessary and beneficial. Other parts of us prefer
to cling to whatever has worked for us in the past. These
conservative inner voices argue, "We've survived so far,
haven't we? Why change something that's working okay?"
These are the aspects of our psyches that urge us to stay
with old patterns that feel safe and comfortable, rather than
risking new things that we're not sure will work.

It is important to acknowledge these seemingly conflicting drives within us in order to understand how they affect
the choices we make in our lives, and how, contrary to what
might be our first impressions, they can actually work together. The tension between the parts of us that want to
grow and change and the parts that want to remain safe in
familiar territory is responsible for triggering what is
called a "healing crisis."

A healing crisis occurs at the point where we have outgrown an old pattern or way of being, but are still unconsciously holding onto that old way because it feels safe and
familiar. Our response to a healing crisis can vary greatly,
both according to who we are and in reaction to other
influences that may be affecting us at the time. We may be
feeling relatively comfortable and content in a pattern that
is no longer vital, unaware that our soul—which always wel-
comes forward motion—is ready to guide us to a new level.
Or we may be feeling stuck and frustrated, wanting to make
a change but not quite willing or able to. So we unconsciously create some kind of physical, emotional, mental, or
spiritual crisis that shakes us out of the old and propels us
into the new.

Healing crises are always uncomfortable and can often
be terrifying and painful. It can feel as if our world is in
danger of coming to an end. It can seem as if our lives are
falling apart. We may see disaster and doom everywhere.
Oftentimes we blame ourselves and feel that we've done

something horribly wrong or that we are, in some way, terribly lacking.

In fact, we have simply outgrown an old form, an old way of relating to the world. An old way of being is dissolving, making way for a new, more expanded and more conscious way. The outer forms in our lives mirror this internal process. So we may lose a job or a relationship because it is too limiting; it would not allow us to expand in the direction we need to go. We may lose a loved one through death because both our souls are moving onto new levels, one of us continuing within the physical body, the other passing into a non-physical reality. We may contract a serious illness in order to confront ourselves with the necessity for change, or confront a choice between continuing our own journey in physical form or moving forward into non-physical reality.

If you have ever gone through crises such as these, and have taken the opportunity to grow from them, you can probably recognize, in retrospect, how vitally important the experience was. From your present vantage point you may even realize that you would never want to return to your previous way of life or level of consciousness.

I know, in my own life, that there have been times, such as during the ending of a relationship, when I experienced a great deal of pain, convinced that my whole world was falling apart. Yet, as I look back at those times and see them in the context of a continuing journey, I can see how necessary they were — more like the opening of doors than the closing of them.

Fortunately, as we progress in the evolution of our consciousness, and we gain more understanding of the growth process, most often we don't have to learn through severe crises. We learn to respond more quickly to the subtler clues that life gives us that it's time for a change! Because we've been through difficult times before and felt the positive results, we have a little more trust. It's easier each time to surrender to change, to let go of the old and open to the new. Still, it's always frightening and difficult to some degree, and we need to have great compassion for ourselves and others who are going through a healing crisis.

A friend of mine had an experience that perfectly illustrates this. She had enjoyed a successful business partnership with a man for many years. Then one day he announced that he wanted to dissolve their partnership and go out on his own. My friend was devastated, feeling that she would never be able to make it without his expertise and support. In the process, she confronted many of her fears and doubts and became aware of certain self-defeating patterns in her behavior. She used the entire process as a learning experience. Today she has a successful business of her own and is very much enjoying her newfound strength and independence. At the time it happened, the change had seemed like a disaster to her, yet it led to healing, growth, and expansion.

I believe that in the Eastern philosophical and spiritual tradition, there is a greater understanding of the process of change and growth than we have in the West. In the Hindu religion, there is a trinity of three main gods—Brahma, the creator, Vishnu, the preserver, and Shiva, the destroyer. In the West, we may find it rather horrifying to worship "The Destroyer" right along with "The Creator." Yet this concept represents a profound understanding of the natural polarities of life—that life includes death and rebirth, and that old forms are constantly being destroyed, making way for the new. In fact, Shiva is the cosmic dancer—the patron of music, dance, and the arts—and they say that his dance keeps the universe in motion.*

* When I was in India, many years ago, I was so profoundly moved by the image and energy of Shiva that I took the name Shakti, which is the feminine form of Shiva. The name of our publishing company, Nataraj, refers to Shiva as the cosmic dancer.

THE WORLD
IN A HEALING CRISIS

---

*Everything that we have been sweeping under
the rug and denying for centuries is coming out
in the open, demanding the birth of a new
awareness. Now is the time to confront the fact
that we are still clinging to patterns of thinking
and behaving that no longer work.*

Just as we may experience a healing crisis on the individual level when we are ready to go through major change and transformation, the same is true on a collective or global level. That is exactly what is happening now. Humanity is making an evolutionary leap in consciousness. And this forward movement of the collective soul is now being experienced throughout the world as a healing crisis on the planetary level.

To fully grasp this, we have to understand how the process of conscious evolution works. As we grow, evolve and expand our consciousness, individually and collectively, the old forms we have created no longer fit. It's as if our awareness is getting bigger, and so it can no longer fit into the forms that used to work. These forms were once quite appropriate; they supported us and allowed us to express ourselves. But now they are no longer working for us. As we grow, it's as if we literally push beyond these old forms that have been containing us. As we step out of them they begin to crumble. They must fall apart to create space for expansion. From that more expanded awareness, we create new, more flexible forms that support us in our new level of consciousness.

On a personal level, we can see this process in action when we lose a job that used to be satisfying but no longer is, or a relationship falls apart that used to feel safe and comfortable but now feels increasingly restrictive. On a collective level we see this process as we watch economic and political systems crumble and institutions fall apart or change drastically. The fall of the Berlin Wall, the dissolution of the Soviet Union, and the shift away from our "cold war" mentality are dramatic examples of this transformational process that we've seen in very recent times. While these might seem like positive changes, it is sometimes more difficult to see our economic crises, violence in our cities, and drug epidemics as an evolution in consciousness. But remember that the old institutions have to crumble to make way for the new. What we are witnessing is the "falling apart" aspect of the process. We are now ready to recognize and acknowledge what didn't work about our old way of doing things, so that we can recreate things in a new and more conscious way.

Both individually and collectively, when we gain new awareness of what's possible, we suddenly look at how we've been doing things, and have a new perspective on our behavior. What seemed perfectly normal up to now may seem very limited, ineffective, or even a bit crazy. It's as if we've found a bit of consciousness to stand on, and this allows us to look back and see our former lack of consciousness.

For example, in your personal life, you may begin to recognize a pattern that you have in a relationship as dysfunctional and self-defeating. You may even find yourself continuing to act out this pattern for awhile, because a part of you is still holding on to the familiar behavior, even though you recognize its limitations and notice how it doesn't really work for you. You can only be having this awareness because another part of you has already recognized that there are other possible ways of behaving. Eventually, you will find yourself shifting into a new, more satisfying way of doing things.

The step of becoming *aware* of our previous patterns and ways of handling life is the most important step in our growth. As a teacher of mine used to say, "90% of change comes from awareness. The other 10% is cleanup."

A woman I know had always been driven by the need to make a lot of money. She was quite successful at this, but she pushed herself relentlessly in order to achieve her goals, working endless hours and sacrificing her personal life and other emotional needs in the process. She entered therapy and began to realize how out of balance her life had become. For about a year, however, she was unable to extricate herself from her driven lifestyle. She was now aware of the pain it caused her, but couldn't bring herself to make any significant changes. Finally, she reduced the hours she was working and began to use her evenings and weekends to rest, nurture herself, and play. Eventually, she took an entire year off, devoting her time to herself and getting in touch with what she really wanted and needed to be happy. During that time, she made some important decisions and discoveries about herself. Today she has a job she loves. She works normal hours, makes less money than before, and enjoys her life!

While we are unconsciously living out our old forms of behavior we may actually numb ourselves to our pain. Then, as we finally shift into the new form of behavior we find ourselves feeling much happier and more satisfied. The truly uncomfortable time is that in-between stage where we are becoming conscious of what doesn't work but are still

caught in the middle of it. It is at this time that whatever we
have been doing to numb ourselves to the pain ceases to
work as well as it once did. And then we discover how much
pain we are really in. As difficult as this might be, it is a
necessary and powerful stage we must go through. We must
have patience and compassion for ourselves, knowing that
real change takes time.

Today we are in this challenging middle stage on a
worldwide level. Many of us are waking up and realizing
that a lot of things in our world aren't working. It's time to
make changes, but we aren't sure yet how to make them.
We're bumbling around, acutely aware of how painful and
destructive our old habits are but not quite knowing what
else to do.

Let's look at the example of war. Down through human
history, in most cultures, war has been seen as inevitable,
natural, an appropriate and effective way to deal with
conflict. But in recent times, increasing numbers of people
are recognizing war as unnecessarily destructive, a bar-
baric and foolish way for human beings to try to solve problems. In fact, to many of us it's starting to look completely
insane. Men and women everywhere are simply refusing to
take part in it or to consider it a viable way to handle any
conflict whatsoever. Yet there continue to be plenty of wars
going on. This is because a large portion of the collective
whole is still operating according to the old pattern; it
doesn't yet know what else to do.

The good news, in my view, is that our collective consciousness is expanding and growing in this and many other
areas. More and more people are becoming aware that we
have fundamental challenges to overcome—in our families,
our educational systems, our cities, our governments, our
economic systems, our international relations, our planetary environment—and that we must find new ways to confront these problems.

Everything that we have been sweeping under the rug and denying for centuries is coming out in the open, demanding the birth of a new awareness. Now is the time to confront the fact that we are still clinging to patterns of thinking and behaving that no longer work. We are beginning to open up, both individually and collectively, to the realization that it is time to create our lives and our world differently. Now is the time for change and transformation.

CREATING REAL CHANGE

Like the proverbial pebble dropped into a still pond, the shifts of consciousness we make in our personal lives send out tiny but important waves that ripple over the surface of the whole.

Most people reading this book will agree that the time has come for profound transformation in our lives and in the world. Indeed, this transformation is already under way. But the question arises, "How can we support and contribute to that process? How can we do our part, as individuals, to make sure it's going in a positive direction? How *do* we create real change in our personal lives and in the world?

The simple answer to that question is this: We change the world most effectively by changing our own consciousness. There is a quote attributed to Mohandas Gandhi that says this well: "You must be the change you wish to see in the world." As each of us becomes more aware on an individual level, we see change reflected in our personal lives. Old problems and patterns gradually melt away and we meet new difficulties and new challenges with a widening perspective and increasing wisdom. Our lives become more balanced, more fulfilling and more in alignment with our

17

soul's purpose. Since each one of us is an integral part of the collective consciousness, we each have a subtle but powerful effect on that mass consciousness (and vice versa). Like the proverbial pebble dropped into a still pond, the shifts of consciousness we make in our personal lives send out tiny but important waves that ripple over the surface of the whole.

When we, as individuals, grow in consciousness, the mass consciousness shifts accordingly. As the mass consciousness changes, it pulls along other individuals who may be clinging to old patterns, or who are simply unaware of how to proceed. So as a few wake up, everyone begins to awaken. And as the collective consciousness expands, the social, economic and political forms of the world change and respond to those new levels of awareness.

I'm sure that many of you reading this book are already familiar with the concept of creating our own reality—the principle that we each take a very active part in creating the kind of world we experience. This metaphysical principle is based on the awareness that everything in the universe is made of one vital element which we can call "energy" or "life force." This being so, everything in life is interconnected. Our thoughts and feelings are a form of energy, as are our physical bodies and seemingly solid material like stone and metal. Many modern physicists, observing this same phenomenon in science, agree that our thoughts, feelings, physical bodies and the material world around us, are all mutually interrelated and constantly affecting one another.

This helps us to understand how we each are constantly creating our own subjective experiences of reality. Our own deepest beliefs and expectations about ourselves, about others, and about life, determine how we perceive external reality, what kinds of people, events and situations we draw to us, and are drawn to, and how we interpret everything that happens to us.

In a very real way, what we experience in our lives is a mirrored image of the values, beliefs, and images we hold within our own consciousness. What we experience shifts considerably as our consciousness changes. One obvious example of this can be seen in people who go into therapy or join twelve-step programs to get out of an addictive pattern of behavior. As they change, their whole circle of friends may change, reflecting new interests and new needs. They become aware of a whole new range of possibilities they couldn't have seen before. They find relationships that are emotionally and spiritually much more fulfilling than anything they were capable of enjoying before. And along with this, their feelings towards themselves change, becoming more positive and self-affirming, raising self-esteem. With greater self-esteem and awareness a whole new world of possibility opens up to them, one that was invisible to them until they changed.

Because our experiences do accurately mirror our inner consciousness, we can actually learn to use our impressions of the external world as reflections of inner selves. Just as looking into the bathroom mirror in the morning allows us to see our faces and physical bodies, so the mirrors provided by our experiences of the external world can allow us to become more aware of our own deepest beliefs, thoughts, and feeling patterns. Using our experiences in the world as mirrors of our inner lives, we can learn what needs to be healed in our own awareness.

Not long ago, a client of mine, who I'll call Jeffrey, became aware that in every one of his jobs he had a difficult time with a domineering, unreasonable co-worker or supervisor. It seemed that such people were always looking over my client's shoulder, telling him every move to make and being both hyper-critical and argumentative. Through first accepting the idea that the experience was a mirrored image of his own consciousness, and then asking what this reflection was revealing to him about himself, he became aware of a pattern established in his own early childhood. He had been raised by a domineering stepfather, a relationship that had been confusing and difficult for him. Through that relationship he had established a deep unconscious emotional pattern that continued to draw him into similar relationships in his adulthood. Once he was able to recognize this, however, and become more aware of his beliefs, feelings and needs around this pattern, the pattern itself shifted.

Along with his new awareness, Jeffrey began to create a new, more harmonious work environment, one in which he no longer got enmeshed with domineering people. Instead of projecting his power onto authority figures, he began to claim his own natural sense of strength. As he owned his own power and authority in a healthy way, others began to treat him with more respect

It is an extremely empowering step on our journey of consciousness, once we can understand that we do in fact create our own reality, and that we can take responsibility for our own life experience. Instead of feeling like a victim of circumstances, or blaming other people for our problems, we can make fuller use of the fact that we each have the creative power of the universe within us.

As we begin working with this mirror concept in our daily lives, it becomes a powerful and trustworthy guide, shining a clear and brilliant light on a path that might otherwise be quite confusing to us. We begin to see the problems that are reflected to us in our lives as graphic illustrations showing us where we are currently unconscious. With this gift of awareness, we can heal and expand our consciousness further. Once we recognize that the difficulties and imbalances in our lives are reflections of our own unconscious patterns, we have a powerful tool to become aware of and change those patterns. After a relatively short period of employing this tool in our lives, we become aware of how much power we actually have to create the lives we truly want.

BLAME
AND RESPONSIBILITY

Choosing to be responsible instead of blaming ourselves is saying, "Yes, I am a powerful, creative being, learning about what it's like to be in physical form, learning how to create. Now that I see and appreciate what I've created, how can I learn from my reality, refine and improve it?"

In recent years, the concept that we create our own reality has gained a great deal of popularity, especially in the New Age movement. Like most principles, the idea that our external reality reflects our internal one can be easily misunderstood. Unfortunately, it is frequently misused and can cause a great deal of unnecessary harm. One woman I heard about refused to go to her doctor when she became seriously ill because she felt so guilty about having somehow "created" this illness. Obviously, this is a terrible, and potentially tragic, misuse of this principle. In this book, I hope to clarify how to use this concept in a healing and empowering way.

It is extremely important to grasp that we are creating our experience of reality in this life not just on the personality level, but from the soul level. In other words, on a deep spiritual level we may be choosing certain circumstances and experiences that contribute to our consciousness growth and development. These may not always feel comfortable or be understandable on the personality level. For example, we might unconsciously choose an illness or other seeming misfortune as the most effective or fastest way to learn, grow, and evolve.

In order to use the mirror of consciousness principle constructively, we need to recognize the difference between responsibility and blame. Many of us have spent our entire lives seeing other people or external circumstances as the cause of our difficulties. Unfortunately, when we finally grasp the concept that we are responsible for our own lives, too many of us begin to *blame* ourselves for the problems that exist in our reality. For example, if I have an illness and I learn that on some level I am creating that reality, I might think, "What's the matter with me that I am creating this illness? If I were a more conscious person I'd be well—or I'd be able to heal myself instantly!" Or, if I am having financial difficulties I might say to myself, "The universe is abundant, so I ought to be able to create prosperity in my own life. There must be something really bad or lacking in me since I am living in poverty."

This kind of self-recrimination is anything but taking responsibility for our lives. Rather, it is self-blame. The peculiar thing about blame is that it actually discourages us from moving forward. And in this respect, the effect is the same whether we are blaming other people or blaming ourselves.

Unfortunately, I see all too many people on the consciousness journey who struggle with this idea of the mirror of consciousness and beat themselves up with blame, not grasping the true meaning of taking responsibility for their realities. When we are blaming ourselves or others, this is fundamentally a disempowering act. It comes from a sense of helplessness and makes us feel worse, actually magnifying that helplessness. Taking responsibility, meanwhile, involves claiming our power to create and change.

Blame is based on the negative assumption that something wrong or bad is happening and therefore someone is in error. Taking an attitude of responsibility, on the other hand, requires us to look at every situation as a potentially valuable learning experience. We need to cultivate the ability to appreciate the reality we've already created, and see the problems in it as gifts that can help us grow and evolve.

We are not to blame for the way our lives are unfolding. Blaming ourselves for our present reality is like blaming a child for being ten years old instead of twenty or thirty. We are evolving in a natural way. We've done the best we knew how up until now. That is one of the ironic things about life, that from moment to moment we have only a limited knowledge about our lives, and we can only make choices and decisions on the basis of what we know. To ask more than that of any human being is as futile and unreasonable as asking a six-month old child to explain what she wants instead of crying. Blaming is a static state, one of standing in place and not moving on, while responsibility—the ability to respond—is dynamic, the very essence of forward movement.

By looking at the reality we have manifested in a "response-able" way, rather than a blaming way, we can learn more. We can become more conscious and aware of our own patterns. Choosing to be responsible instead of blaming ourselves is saying, "Yes, I am a powerful, creative being, learning about what it's like to be in physical form, learning how to create. Now that I see and appreciate what I've created, how can I learn from my reality, refine and improve it?"

As we do our consciousness work, spiritually and psychologically, we become more and more aware of our own deeply held assumptions and belief systems about life, and our habitual emotional patterns and reactions. We can begin to see how these factors of our "inner reality" shape and influence our experience of what we commonly think of as "external realty." We find that as we heal our emotional wounds and change our beliefs, the experiences of our lives change, sometimes almost miraculously. We begin to have a real experience of how we are creating our own personal reality.

Many times, in workshops, with my clients, and in my own private life, I have seen this kind of transformation occur. I am thinking now of a young woman, who I'll call Althea, who attended a workshop I gave in Los Angeles. Althea had not spoken to her sister for years, owing to a conflict they'd had in their early twenties. During the workshop, Althea realized she had been clinging to her old pattern of blaming and feeling like a victim, and the only thing it ever got her was a feeling of sadness over not having her sister's friendship anymore. She was able to express and release the feelings that were keeping her separated from her sister, and in the process felt greatly relieved.

During the lunch break, Althea called her office to check for phone messages. One of the messages was from her sister. Althea called her back and discovered that her sister, also, had gone through a similar healing process of her own. When Althea returned to the workshop, she shared this story with us, saying how grateful she was to be able to be close to her sister again. Seemingly, their relationship had been healed across the miles in the instant that Althea saw the old pattern of blame and was able to let go of it.

Once we are able to embrace this concept of creating our own reality, it becomes quite easy to embrace the concept that we also participate in creating the world reality. It can be helpful to think of everyone's individual consciousness being as active and alive in the collective consciousness as are the billions of beings who make up the life of the sea. Just as we are each creating our individual reality, the mass consciousness is creating the collective reality. Whatever attitudes and beliefs are held most deeply and powerfully in the mass consciousness will, for better or worse, be manifested in the collective reality of the world. Unresolved conflict and pain, held in the consciousnesses of millions of people the world over can, and I believe does, get reflected back to us in war, violence in our cities, and in our collective disregard for the rights of other human beings and the well-being of the Earth.

As the mass consciousness evolves, the collective experience of reality gradually changes. We see evolution taking place in physical form in our world through new ideas, changing religious beliefs, the emergence of new social and political systems, and the development of new technologies. Our world as it is today is a clear and accurate reflection of our present collective consciousness.

It is, I believe, absolutely critical that we understand and learn to more fully appreciate how our evolution as individuals automatically changes the collective consciousness of our world. While we might feel that we are mere drops in a vast ocean of consciousness, the interesting thing is that the evolution of each "mere drop" is a tremendously powerful force. It takes a relatively small number of souls moving into alignment with universal forces to have a great impact on our global reality.

We must never underestimate the potent impact we each have on the collective consciousness, whether we are taking responsibility for it or not. As we cultivate our own consciousness growth process, we affect others profoundly and we spur forward the mass consciousness in its evolution. Through our individual efforts we truly can change the world. This is happening even as you sit here reading this book.

Interestingly, since we're integrally connected in consciousness, no one individual can evolve far ahead of everyone else. We are all contained within a certain force field of consciousness. Though we may take a role close to the leading edge, we cannot leave our fellow beings far behind since in essence we are all one. So we have no choice but to evolve together, bringing all our brothers and sisters along with us.

TAKING ACTION

We begin to see here, that for our personal or social/political actions to be most effective, we need to start with a deep understanding and commitment to our own consciousness process.

As we discuss how we can make real change through our consciousness, the question naturally arises, "Are we supposed to just sit around, trying to get conscious and somehow that's going to improve our lives and the world? Don't we have to take action in order to make our lives work, and don't we need to get involved in social and political activities in order to deal with the very real problems and challenges that exist in the world?"

Of course, taking action is a vital part of bringing our consciousness into form and making real change. Direct, powerful, and committed action is extremely important both on a personal and social/political level. Whether or not we commit ourselves to such actions is not so much the issue as where the motivation for that action comes from within us.

The pitfall is this: If we put our *primary* attention and commitment into external action, we repeat an old pattern, one that is at the root of much of the trouble we're in today—which is believing that the cause of the problem, as well as the power to correct it, exists primarily in the external world.

If we try to solve our problems only externally, which we often do by trying to fix or change other people or institutions, we give away our power. We project it *out there*, into the external world instead of owning where it really exists, and where we can actually do something about it—inside us.

For example, many people who were active in the womens' movement, and who worked very hard to change male dominance in our society came to the point of a personal impasse in their forties or fifties. Clearly they had helped to change our society for the better, but they found they could move ahead in their personal lives only after confronting in themselves some of the same gender biases they had been fighting in the external world. This phenomenon was well-documented in Gloria Steinem's book *Revolution From Within: A Book of Self-Esteem.**

When our primary focus is to go out and try to change things in the external world, we may accomplish some of our goals, but ultimately our effectiveness will be pretty limited. Time and time again history has shown, for instance, that settling border disputes between countries through the use of force, that is, by one country using the threat of violence to impose their beliefs and their needs on another, may bring temporary change but inevitably leads to new disputes and conflicts. Political scientists have often said that some of the bloodiest wars in human history have been fought because one group became convinced that there could be peace only if their neighbors, or the rest of the world, agreed with them and fully adopted their beliefs.

Lasting change comes only when we get completely away from thinking that the core problem is *out there* somewhere, that our peace of mind can only be won by changing

---

* Published by Little, Brown, New York, 1992.

others. The kind of thinking that we must change in ourselves is the belief that it's somebody else's fault, it's those
other people, it's that situation, it's that other country, that
other race, that government, those politicians, or it's those
unconscious people, who are responsible for the way things
are. We need to let go of this way of thinking not just
because it's a *nice* or *spiritually aware* thing to do, but
because it is the only way we can discover and take responsibility for our own power.

Where do we begin? We begin by first understanding
and fully embracing the awareness that all those people and
institutions reflect aspects of ourselves. They are manifestations of our own consciousness and the process that is
going on inside us at this very moment. When we take this
kind of responsibility—and believe me, it is one of the biggest responsibilities we will ever assume—we say with con-
viction that, "Yes, I can understand how this situation
reflects a part of my own inner conflict. I can see how these
people mirror aspects of me. I can see how these things that
are going on in the world may reflect things that are going
on in my own life. I take responsibility (not blame) for what
I see."

Once we accept this responsibility to hold our power
within ourselves and we see the world as mirroring aspects
of ourselves, then we can take a particular kind of external
action that will be extremely effective. This kind of action
begins with owning our center of power and responsibility
within ourselves.

It is only from that place of power and responsibility
that we can put our energy into action, supporting our
awareness. We need to walk our talk. We need to say what
we honestly feel, and act on what we know. We need to talk
about, act upon, give our time, energy, and money to causes
we believe in. We need to live our truth as fully as possible,
every moment of our lives.

Deena Metzger, author of *Writing for Your Life*, works with people to help them achieve what she calls "personal disarmament." She sees the inner life of the individual as being much like a nation-state, one that contains multiple selves, governed as countries are governed. Problems and issues that afflict nations also affect our own "inner countries." Sometimes the citizens of this nation state of the psyche live in harmony and peace; at other times they may be in rebellion, fighting one another. We need to be able to recognize the different interests and needs of these various selves, to sometimes negotiate agreements with them, and to not keep one group or the other buried, or hidden away. What's perhaps even more important, we need to recognize what kind of inner government we have: Dictatorial and repressive? Laissez-faire to the point of laxness? Openly democratic, allowing each self to have its say?

The nation-state of the self doesn't just keep to itself, isolated from others. Rather, that inner state interacts with the outer world in ways that affect the world just as much as real nations do. We project our inner conflicts, our rebellions, repressions, and fears, to the outside world all the time. I have found it helpful to look at our inner worlds in this way—to identify what kind of inner governments we have, what inner selves we allow to openly express and enjoy themselves, and what inner selves we repress and try to hold down.

As a political liberal I used to feel irritated and judgmental toward people with a conservative viewpoint. Now I recognize that they represent a conservative side of my own inner nation-state that I am less in touch with than my liberal side. Recently, while visiting a friend's family, her brother began to express opinions which I strongly disagreed with, having to do with a local environmental issue. Rather than jumping immediately into a highly polarized argument, I paused to acknowledge my annoyance inwardly and to remind myself that this person was mirroring a part of me—a citizen of my own inner nation—that I have trouble accepting. After that I was able to make a few clear points from my own perspective which at least gave him something to think about without needlessly antagonizing him.

If I'm able to see someone in my life as a reflection of myself, and then have the courage to speak my truth to that person when appropriate, while simultaneously recognizing that part of myself they are mirroring to me, I'm taking responsibility for the whole process. I'm speaking and living my truth. And there is no way that I can be more effective either in the external world or in my inner life.

We begin to see here, that for our personal or social/political actions to be most effective, we need to start with a deep understanding and commitment to our own consciousness process. This begins by recognizing that we truly do have a strong influence on creating the realities we experience, that we tend to draw to us those people and experiences that reflect our own consciousness in some way.

Working from that base, we can learn what it is to take action from our own deepest inner sense of truth. We can discover the power of doing what we genuinely feel moved to do, what our hearts tell us is the right thing to do. Too often we base our actions on external standards or rules of behavior we've blindly adopted. Or we take a particular path of action because it seems like a rational idea or a theoretically good course to pursue.

Some years ago, I met a psychiatrist in his mid-forties who had come to a major turning point in his life over this very issue. His life was literally falling apart, and he no longer wanted to see patients. He said he was tired of hearing about people's problems, largely because he was convinced that he wasn't helping them in any way.

As he began questioning his own motives, he quickly saw that he had never really felt any great urge to become a doctor. In fact, the decision to go to medical school was one he'd made when he was still a teenager. It was a decision based on neither his knowledge of what psychiatrists do, nor on anything that came from his own heart. It was a decision based primarily on the fact that his best friend had chosen to study psychiatry and his own parents had been enthusiastic and supportive of the idea.

This man had been wise enough to recognize that he had little to offer his patients except what he had learned in his medical training; nothing was coming from his heart. His feelings of impotence, reflected by his belief that he was not helping his patients, was coming from something he felt within him—that he was not operating from his own inner truth.

A couple of years later, I learned that this man had sold his practice and was working part-time in an emergency room, putting most of his time and energy into pursuing his own consciousness journey. He had written two articles for magazines on controversial topics and had gotten lots of lively reactions. He was feeling very excited about the possibility of using his writing skills to make a difference in the world.

When we look at our own lives, or the lives of friends and acquaintances, it is easy to see that this man is by no means alone in his search. His is just one example among perhaps millions showing that we need to follow not just what our heads would tell us are appropriate actions, but what we feel in our guts. We need to be asking what it is that enlivens, empowers, excites us, turns us on, makes us genuinely feel satisfied and fulfilled. That's what actually heals us, and heals the world.

Even in the political world there are examples of whole societies or nations that have followed their hearts in the way I'm describing. During the second World War, for example, the people of Norway, as well as the citizens of a small settlement called Mondragon in the Basque area of Spain, refused to cooperate with the Fascist takeovers of their regions. Following the truths of their own hearts, they were guided to find ways not only to resist the violent military machine that was sweeping Europe, but to do so with little bloodshed as well. They ended up strengthening their own resolve to create societies which even today are some of the most productive, wealthy, and humane in the whole world. More recently, we have seen in Russia examples of the soldiers who refused to fire upon their own people when their superior officers ordered them to. In the end, it was those who followed their hearts and supported the democratic uprising of that country who made the greatest difference. Even all the military might of one of the world's greatest powers could not stop them.

We have the greatest healing effect on the world when we allow the life force to move through our own bodies. Our power comes not simply by what we say or do. Rather, our words and actions are vehicles for our life energy. What really transforms is the life force moving through us.

When you are in touch with your inner truth and you walk into a room, you may have an impact on the lives of everyone there simply because you have so much life force moving through you. You need not even say or do anything, other than simply being there. On some level, conscious or unconscious, people feel this and are affected by it. It stimulates their own life energy and begins to trigger change and growth for them. It may catalyze some type of healing crisis in their lives. And so they experience growth as a result, and you have contributed to the healing of this planet, probably without even knowing it.

A friend of mine told me an interesting story. A few years ago, she committed herself to a process of emotional healing and recovery from addiction. As a result of her example, her brother also got deeply involved in his healing process. He recently told her that he had gone back to their hometown in New England to find at least twenty of their friends involved in similar processes of recovery, healing, and growth, all as a direct or indirect result of the influence of my friend and her brother.

Having seen examples of these phenomena many, many times over the years, I am convinced that our commitment to our own growth and healing processes serves as a catalyst for countless others — our family, our friends, and even people whose names we may never know. The power of being committed to the truths of our own hearts releases energy into our own bodies and into the world that can heal some of the most grievous and long-standing troubles of the world.

How exactly does all this work? How does commitment to the truths of their heart in one person ripple through entire communities like this? We don't really know how it happens, but it is clear that it does — and much more often than we might think. The fact that it happens at all suggests that the concept of oneness, that we are all one, is indeed a fact of life, not just an obscure spiritual abstraction. Our own thoughts, feelings, and actions are not isolated occurrences taking place within the confines of our own bodies, but are in fact manifestations of the one spiritual and energetic source that moves through every one of us. It is no more possible for one of us to change without changing the rest as it is for a single wave to crest in the ocean without affecting the whole.

The Consciousness Journey

Consciousness is not a destination at which we finally arrive. It is an ongoing, ever-deepening, infinitely expanding process, a journey that perhaps has no end.

A t this point you might ask, "If the way to create real change in my life and in the world is primarily through my own consciousness growth, what exactly does that mean? What is consciousness growth?"

Let us begin with a statement that may at first seem quite obvious — that consciousness is awareness and understanding, while unconsciousness is a lack of the same. Consciousness growth, then, is the process of becoming aware of things we were formerly unaware of. It is really as simple as that.

Consciousness growth happens naturally as a part of every being's evolution. For example, a baby's consciousness grows as she becomes aware of her fingers and toes and learns how to move them and play with them. A man grows in consciousness when, as a result of a serious illness and a decision to regain his health, he learns that certain foods and behaviors can help that process along while others can actually be quite detrimental.

In our society, consciousness is generally associated with the mind, that is, "improving your mind," or gaining mental skills that allow you to perform a particular task better or "know more" in order to pass a test, get a higher degree in college or become an expert in a certain field. However, in the sense that we are discussing it here, our consciousness growth involves our four levels of existence — the spiritual, the mental, the emotional and the physical.

So we might attend college, for example, in order to become more aware and knowledgeable about a particular subject. But we might not realize that in the process of attending school we may be developing at many other levels as well, raising our self-esteem, perhaps, and discovering more about our soul's purpose.

Life is fundamentally a journey of consciousness, a journey of growing awareness. However, most of us aren't fully aware of this evolutionary process of our lives, nor do we understand in depth how it works. Therefore, most people are as yet *unconsciously* involved in a process of consciousness growth!

We make a great leap forward when we recognize the evolutionary nature of our lives and begin to understand how it works. As this awareness increases, we can choose to embrace our own lives as a consciousness process, and make a commitment to that process, to keep it in focus and do whatever we can to move through it much more rapidly. By doing so, most people enjoy their lives more, finding deeper fulfillment and satisfaction than ever before.

Making a commitment to your consciousness growth means making a decision to become aware of and understand as much as you can about yourself, others, life, and the universe. It involves looking at life as a learning experience in which every single thing that happens to us can be seen as a potential gift to help us develop our full potential.

One ironic thing about the consciousness journey is that with every new step we take, we become aware of things we

were unaware of before. Facing our previous unconsciousness can be very difficult and unpleasant. Until we become
comfortable with the journey itself, seeing that over time
our lives do become more fulfilled by following such a path,
the discovery of what we don't know can cause us to feel
quite fearful. As humans, we like to believe that we know
where we stand at any given moment. We like to feel that our
beliefs are complete or "right" or unquestionable. Most people on a consciousness journey, however, learn that our
awareness is constantly changing and that as consciousness
evolves there is a peace of mind and security that comes
with letting go of the need to be right. So, one of the first
things we learn as we embark on this journey is the willingness to face our unconsciousness.

Like a light in the darkness, our awareness automatically illuminates areas where we have not been aware. Until
we are able to stop criticizing or castigating ourselves for
our ignorance, our journey cannot move along freely. It is a
process that flourishes in a spirit of acceptance, compassion and adventure. We need to see ourselves much as we
see young children who are growing and learning. In a
sense, we are all children in an evolutionary process, moving as quickly as it is appropriate for us to go. And we must
always bear in mind that there is much more to learn than
any of us can learn in a single lifetime.

One thing very important to understand is that *the consciousness journey is lifelong*. In fact, it is most likely many
lives long. But certainly it will continue throughout our
present lifetime. Consciousness is not a destination at
which we finally arrive. It is an ongoing, ever-deepening,
infinitely expanding process, a journey that perhaps has no
end.

Because we live in a quick-fix, meal-in-a-minute, product-
oriented society, I feel it is very important to emphasize the
lifelong, ever-evolving nature of the consciousness journey.
It is important to understand that it is a process rather than

a product. All too many teachers and healers espouse the idea that there is a specific destination or defined goal that we're seeking. Too many promise that "enlightenment" can be had, once and for all, simply by following their prescription, that if you read this book, attend this workshop, practice this meditation, follow this diet or this program, your life will be healed, your problems cured, miracles will happen, and you'll never again have any difficulties in your life.

The product-oriented approach to consciousness is very appealing to the part of us that yearns for an instant remedy, a magic recipe. We don't want to go through any pain or discomfort. We quickly grow impatient with self-examination. We don't want to take the time to find our own path. We want an all-knowing, all-powerful parent figure to give us answers and tell us exactly what to do. We want a spiritual white knight to sweep us up and carry us away from the trials and tribulations of being human. We want to pack our bags and fly away into a never-never land of enlightenment, the quicker the better.

Unfortunately, it simply doesn't happen this way. The journey of a human being is much more complex than this, and involves an intense willingness to embrace all aspects of life. We don't find our way by avoiding, skipping over, or running away from anything.

I warn against these promised shortcuts and miracle cures not because I think the consciousness journey should be difficult but because there are actual hazards in pursuing instant enlightenment. At the top of the list of such hazards is that when we are offered such promises and they don't work, we usually blame ourselves. Over the years I have encountered far too many people in the personal growth movement who are beating themselves up because they think something is wrong with them. They have been on a consciousness journey for many years now, and they feel they should be far more evolved than they seem to be. They still have relationship problems, health problems, work problems. They've attended prosperity workshops, have said their prosperity affirmations faithfully, but they're still having financial difficulties. They know they create their own reality, yet they haven't managed to heal themselves. They've followed a spiritual teacher for years, yet they're not feeling very enlightened. They are filled with doubt and possibly are becoming quite disillusioned, but most end up asking themselves, "What's wrong with me?"

The answer is that there is nothing wrong with them. Like the rest of us, they are human beings on an ongoing, lifelong journey. Consciousness growth is a challenging process, one that involves us both individually and collectively. Our own evolution affects the larger whole, the consciousness of the planet, and the evolution of that whole affects us. Every time we move to a new level of awareness—individually or collectively—we are confronted with new areas of denial, ignorance, pain, and, ultimately, healing. The process moves in cycles, so at times we feel clear and powerful, and at other times we feel lost in confusion. At times we feel stuck, being challenged to move ever more deeply into a specific area of healing. We struggle and resist for a time but when we can finally embrace those aspects of ourselves that we're resisting, we move quickly through them, finally at peace again for a time.

I'm not denying that miracles do happen. They do! Sometimes a specific workshop, or therapy session, or meditation provides a breakthrough; something shifts and our lives are never again the same. Sometimes, a shift occurs for no apparent reason at all—it's just time. We can enjoy and appreciate such wonderful moments of change and growth. But we need to understand them for what they are—powerful steps on an infinite and fascinating journey.

It's important to know, also, that the journey consists of many different kinds of steps. Tools or techniques that are helpful and appropriate at one place in the journey may not be effective in the next. We may need to find a different approach than we've ever tried before. Once we've mastered a certain principle or teaching, we don't usually get to rest on our laurels for very long! Life keeps pushing us to the next area of growth, which may require a very different understanding.

For example, you may have learned to meditate deeply, and know how to find your center in the midst of emotional upheaval and external chaos. This ability may serve you well at a certain time in your life. And you may come to a different time in your life, when this approach no longer feels right or is simply no longer effective. It may be time to explore feelings and express your emotions, or to risk taking more direct action in the world. Whatever our next step is, life has a way of pushing, pulling, and prodding us toward it, by any means necessary!

I think of periods in my own life when the most important lesson of the time was to learn how to let go, to let go of an old belief and make room for something new, or to let go of a close friendship or lover. At another time, the lesson would seem to be just the opposite, to learn how to hold my ground, to stand up for the beliefs that were true for me, or to do everything I could to work through difficulties I was having with another person in my life.

The journey of consciousness is a spiral. We move in cycles, but each cycle takes us to a deeper level. When we find a familiar lesson coming around again, we should never jump to the conclusion that it's coming up because we didn't learn it the first time around. Instead, we need to remind ourselves that we are always moving into deeper levels of awareness that cause us to take a new and different look at what may seem, at first glance, to be the same old issue.

It's helpful to see our consciousness growth process as an adventure, perhaps the ultimate one. We don't know where it's going to take us, but on some deep level we know that it's going to be worthwhile. Sometimes the going gets rough or turns into just plain drudgery. At other times it's easy and fun. There are moments of clarity and inspiration. And there are moments that are dark and scary. The important thing is not to focus on the destination, being at peace with the fact that there isn't any final end point. *We need to become fascinated with the journey itself,* so that every moment in the process of learning, growth, and expansion becomes its own rich reward.

A COSMIC PERSPECTIVE
ON LIFE

The time has come for the reunion and integration of male and female principles into a balanced and harmonious form. This is now in the process of taking place, and this is why it's very exciting to be alive on this planet right now!

In order to clarify the consciousness process as I see it, I'd like to take a step back and give you a cosmic perspective of the universe, life on earth, why we are here, what we are doing, and what it's all about!

There are many different levels of reality in the universe, many different realms of existence. The physical plane is only one of those realms. On the purely spiritual plane, we are all a part of one infinite intelligent life force. In other realms we may exist as individual entities, still very aware of and connected to our oneness. We exist in all these realms simultaneously. Those of us who are currently focused in physical reality touch into the other realms through our nightly dreams, through prayer and meditation, and sometimes through psychic or "paranormal" experiences.

The physical plane is the most dense realm of existence. It's solid and slow compared with other levels where creation and impulse are often one and the same. On the dense physical plane time becomes an important factor, taking hours, days, months, years, or even decades to bring things into physical form. I believe that the physical plane was created in order to fully explore and develop our creative power. It is a plane of duality where all things exist as polarities.

One way to think of it is this: The oneness wanted to explore "two-ness," or "otherness." It wanted to develop its opposite. Or to phrase it more poetically, the universe wanted to make love to itself, so it created the physical world in order to develop separation and reunion.

So physical reality can be viewed as a place of exploration and discovery, in a constant creative, evolutionary process. We are all divine, eternal beings, aspects of the essential oneness of life. As such, we have chosen to focus our attention and awareness here in physical reality for a time, in order to learn, grow, and develop, in order to give something to and receive something from the experience.

Since the material plane is so dense, it is a difficult and challenging place for a spiritual entity to hang out. We might well think of ourselves as the gambler/adventurers of the universe—the cosmic risk-takers. I can almost hear a conversation between two entities contemplating coming into physical form:

"Hey, want to do Earth? I hear it's a real heavy trip. Let's see if we can handle it!"

"Okay, I'm up for a challenge. How about if we meet there in about 30 Earth years?"

Then they get in here on the physical plane, feel the density, and they start thinking: "Oh, my God, what have I done? Get me out of here!"

I'm joking about this, of course, but in fact a large number of people I meet have a strong basic yearning to leave their physical bodies and return to another less dense realm. I believe this is because the journey of physical existence is inherently quite difficult. Yet there is great learning to be had here, and the possibility of incredible rewards and satisfactions, or we wouldn't be here doing this.

The first major experience to be explored on the physical plane is that of individuality, limitation, and separation, i.e., the opposite of the essential spiritual experience of oneness and limitlessness. Because the experience of oneness is already so powerful, we've needed to develop its opposite principle — individuality — equally strongly. Another way to think of this is that the feminine principle (spirit) was already fully developed; we needed to birth and develop the male principle (form) to match her power so that we could ultimately experience their union.*

It's taken us a few million years of earthly existence to develop and strengthen this male principle of separation, individuality, and self-expression. We've developed it to the point that it now balances the feminine. If we continue to go in the direction we've been traveling, however, we will have gone too far, destroying our physical existence altogether. The time has come for the reunion and integration of male and female principles into a balanced and harmonious form. This is what is happening now, and this is why it's very exciting to be alive on this planet right now!

---

* I describe this concept in greater detail in my book, *Return to the Garden*.

THE PATH
OF THE MATERIAL WORLD

Down through history, a majority of human beings have been focusing on what I call the path of the material world—the process of learning to survive and succeed in the physical realm.

For most of us in the Western world, being born into a physical body has resulted in our forgetting about our spiritual origins. Our primary task has been to explore this dense realm of the physical world and develop a sense of ourselves as unique individuals. If we had remained strongly conscious of the spiritual level of our existence, the pull of the oneness experience might have been too powerful and compelling, and we might not have wanted to remain focused here. So we developed a mechanism of denial to shut out our connection to our essential being.

Unfortunately, the mechanisms we've developed to shut out our sense of oneness have left us each feeling fundamentally alone in the universe, lost and empty. However, it clearly has allowed us to concentrate on the work we set out to do here—to survive and develop as individuals on the physical plane. To do this we each had to develop a unique physical body and personality. And the lost, empty, lonely feelings we experienced have provided a perfect driving force to move us out into life—discovering, developing, creating—in an effort to find satisfaction and fulfillment.

Down through history, a majority of human beings have been focusing on what I call the path of the material world—the process of learning to survive and succeed in the physical realm. In order to do this, we have had to mostly disconnect from awareness of any other level of our being and lose ourselves in the world of physical form, believing in its reality more than any other. This has been painful, but a necessary evolutionary step. In a sense we have all sacrificed our deeper happiness in order to fulfill this mission.

I want to emphasize that there is nothing wrong with being materially oriented. It is a very necessary and important stage in our individual growth process and our human evolution. We have needed to discover, experience, and develop the many aspects of our lives as human beings fully participating on the physical plane. A vast majority of humanity today is primarily focused on this fascinating process.

Many of us who are now on consciousness journeys began this lifetime by following the path of the material world, but at some point we have sensed that other alternatives exist, and we have begun our spiritual reawakening.

THE PATH
OF TRANSCENDENCE

While it may help to remind us that our physical existence is not all there is, the transcendent path does tend to create a growing chasm between spirit and form, between who we are as spiritual beings and who we are as human personalities in physical bodies.

In recent history, it seems that the majority of people have been mainly focused on the path of the material world, developing skills necessary for physical existence. Meanwhile, there has always been a small number of individuals who have taken a very different path. Whether guided by religious practices of the East or the West, this latter group—including monks, nuns, priests, yogis, rabbis, and other types of spiritual leaders, as well as solitary ascetics or simply faithful devotees—has focused primarily on remembering and developing their awareness of the spiritual level of being. In doing so, they have played an important role in the evolution of our planet, maintaining our connection with spirit. So from the perspective of the mass consciousness, we have all been working together—the majority focusing on mastering the physical world, while the few held our link to the spiritual realm.

For each individual, however, there has been a kind of split, a choice to be made between form and spirit. We could either be worldly or we could be spiritual, but we couldn't be both. Or so it was believed!

In both the Eastern and Western traditions, there have been the belief and the implication that to focus on the spiritual path you must renounce the world. Were you to be truly committed to a spiritual life, you had to stay as far as you could from the "worldly" aspects of life, such as relationships (especially sexual or emotionally intimate ones), business, money, and material possessions. All these things were seen as temptations, attachments that hook us into worldly involvement and draw us away from the spiritual focus. From the traditional spiritual perspective, the only solution to the apparent conflict between these two realities was to commit to spirit and minimize our involvement with the material world. The ultimate goal was to leave the limited world of form by leaving our physical bodies, thus returning fully to the realm of spirit.

I call this traditional spiritual approach the "path of transcendence." It focuses on a very important step in the evolution of consciousness — remembering that we are not simply physical forms, lost in and limited by the material world, but are in essence unlimited, eternal spiritual beings, a part of the oneness of all life. This is a vitally important and beautiful step that all of us must make at some time. Remembering the essence of who we are, that we exist beyond our physical form, gives us a much clearer perspective on our lives and on our human problems. It allows us to transcend the apparent limitations of human form and reclaim our true place in the universe. I believe it is primarily a search for this perspective that led so many in our culture to experiment with psychedelic drugs in the '60s, and has motivated so many westerners in recent years to study traditional Eastern philosophies and practices such as meditation. This yearning for spiritual transcendence has also given rise to many of the New Age philosophies and groups that have developed in recent times.

However, like any stage in the development of consciousness, the path of transcendence can have its own problems and limitations if we don't move on to the next step. To a great degree, the transcendent spiritual philosophies and practices have been a *reaction* to the pain and limitation of feeling stuck and imprisoned in the world of the material plane. While it may help to remind us that our physical existence is not all there is, the transcendent path does tend to create a growing chasm between spirit and form, between who we are as spiritual beings and who we are as human personalities in physical bodies.

The transcendent spiritual view is that the physical world is fundamentally unreal, an illusion in which we have become imprisoned. Our human bodies and personalities are traps from which we must escape to find true liberation in the higher realms. Therefore, we must strive to transcend our human experience, our physical and emotional needs, our feelings and passions. Ultimately we want to leave our physical bodies and the physical world so that we can merge with pure spirit, in oneness.

This philosophy seems to imply that the physical plane is just a big mistake, or perhaps a type of hell or purgatory through which we must pass, learning the error of our ways before we are allowed to get back where we really belong. There's the implication—and sometimes overt claim—that life here on earth is inherently inferior to what our existence can be in the higher realms. The experience of individuality we have here is seen as negative; we simply need to get back as fast as possible to the experience of pure oneness. There's often a feeling that there's something wrong with us for being here on the physical plane, that we are lesser beings than those inhabiting other realms.

It is my belief that this system of thought ignores the obvious fact that this physical realm has been created for a reason, and that on some level we've chosen to be here rather than remain solely on the spiritual plane. Regardless of how it may look and feel sometimes, there's something very powerful and exciting happening here. The physical world is not just some big mistake on the part of Creative Intelligence—God's goof! Somehow, I'm quite convinced that we didn't just come here in order to see how quickly we could escape. There's a unique experience of infinite value and richness to be had here if we're willing to see and embrace it.

For many people currently following a transcendent philosophy, the term "ego" has become almost a dirty word. One hears a great deal of talk in the New Age movement, for example, about "getting rid of," or "letting go of" the ego. The ego is designated as our enemy, the part that tries to keep us from embracing our spiritual awareness—and any effort to even suggest that the ego has any value is seen as nothing more than the ego fighting to justify itself. Unfortunately, this belief simply deepens the confusion and fear. It's a bit like attributing anything we don't like to the "work of the devil."

By treating the ego as our enemy, we unwittingly create an adversarial thought system, a belief that there are "good parts" and "bad parts" within us, and we have to weed out the latter. Ironically, this is a form of blaming that keeps us searching for someone or something to blame and sets up false conflicts.

The idea that we have something to gain by getting rid of the ego is based on a misunderstanding of the ego's actual function. Our egos are simply our awareness of ourselves as individuals. The term "ego" can be roughly equated with the term "personality." It is that aspect of our consciousness that is concerned with our survival and well-being on the physical plane.

There is nothing inherently good or bad about the ego; it is simply a fact of life, like the physical body. And without an ego, we could not survive for a moment in the physical realm. So if we get rid of the ego, we have to leave our body. The attempt to suppress our ego simply deepens the split and intensifies the conflict between spirit and form. Any time we try to get rid of or deny a part of ourselves or a part of life, we get into terrible conflicts in which the denied aspect starts fighting for its very existence! So, of course, we experience the ego as "resisting" our attempt to get rid of it.

A far less contradictory or frustrating approach, and one that is much more productive, is to understand that the function of ego is to ensure our survival as an individual with a physical form. Rather than fruitlessly attempting to annihilate our egos, we need to appreciate them for what they are and foster cooperation between ego and spirit. We can then *educate* our egos to the fact that opening to our spiritual essence can actually enhance our lives on Earth. We can develop an aware ego or conscious personality that embraces our spiritual energy and views our human existence within the larger universal perspective.

Very few people on the path of transcendence ever fully achieve their avowed goal—a kind of "enlightenment" which involves becoming almost totally identified with one's spiritual self and mostly disowning one's human feelings and needs—i.e., "ego." Those who have done so, such as many Christian saints and martyrs, often have died at an early age, frequently with much physical suffering, stemming, I believe, from the denial of the physical body.

So-called enlightened masters who have achieved some level of transcendence can be fascinating teachers, especially when we are just embarking on a consciousness journey and are needing inspiration and a powerful source of guidance and authority. However, most transcendent masters or saints, having denied the world, can only live in relative seclusion, surrounded by devotees who care for their earthly needs and protect them, at least to some extent, from having to deal with everyday practicalities. And unfortunately, they all too often prove to have feet of clay, i.e., at least some human tendencies that keep stubbornly reappearing (although usually in secret). Most often these involve the very energies that they and their followers have been trying hard to transcend—sexuality, aggression, and the desire for money and worldly possessions.

Throughout history there have been scandals and tragedies surrounding the emergence of the repressed "shadow" side of transcendent spiritual leaders. So we have the "celibate" priests, nuns, and yogis, or the married fundamentalist ministers, who are discovered to have secret lovers; most often these illicit sexual encounters are with their own followers, who are overly trusting and dependent. Other examples of the problem range from church leaders who are corrupted by financial greed, to tragic incidents such as the Jonestown disaster at Guyana, or the fiery deaths of the Branch Davidians near Waco, Texas.

The vast majority of seekers on the path of transcendence never make it anywhere near so-called "enlightenment," and relatively few find much peace or self-acceptance. I'm afraid that most people who choose the transcendent path eventually find themselves mired down in the apparent split between the physical and the spiritual—torn between the needs of the soul and the desires of the ego. Try as they might to subdue their humanness and rise above it, they often find themselves battling with conflicting parts of themselves. Sometimes, even after years of meditation and other spiritual practices, they find themselves filled with self-criticism, feeling like failures. Instead of achieving the enlightened state they seek, they end up chastising themselves for not being further along in their spiritual development.

The transcendent path does very little to address the problems of the physical world. Indeed, it regards the material plane as an illusion or dream from which we need to awaken—or escape! More often than not, those on a transcendent path literally abandon the physical world. They treat everything that happens in that realm as an illusion, not to be taken seriously in any way. After all, if our commitment is to try to transcend the world, how could we find any value in trying to transform it?

We can see the results of narrowly limiting ourselves to either the material path or the transcendent path by looking at the Western industrialized countries, where the material path is fiercely pursued, and many of the Eastern countries where the transcendent path has been pursued just as strongly. Devoted almost exclusively to material development, the Western cultures have developed a technology so advanced that we now have the power to destroy our world—if not through atomic weaponry, then through pollution. In many Eastern or Third World countries, where there are very strong spiritual traditions, there has been a tendency to focus on the transcendent energies to the point where physical existence falls into neglect, chaos, and extreme poverty.

It is important to understand that the path of the material world and the path of transcendence each has its place in our individual development and in the evolution of human consciousness. However, neither of them alone offers us what we need to meet the many challenges we face today in our personal and planetary lives. For this reason it concerns me to see so many people today who are involved in the human potential or New Age movements still attempting to follow an essentially transcendental philosophy. In order to truly heal our lives and change the world we need to take another step—onto the path of transformation.

THE PATH
OF TRANSFORMATION

*Through lovingly embracing the full range of
our experience—human and divine—we can
heal the split that has existed between spirit and
form, in ourselves individually and in the whole
world. We can bring the full power and awareness of our spiritual beings into our human lives
and all our worldly endeavors.*

A t this time in our evolution we have an exciting new way
to focus our consciousness journey. I call it the path of
transformation. Rather than being limited by physical reality, as on the path of the material world, or seeking to
escape the physical form so we can return to the realm of
spirit, as on the transcendent path, the path of transformation challenges us to create an entirely new reality. This new
reality is created not by denying either the physical or the
spiritual but, on the contrary, by integrating the two. It is a
path that can lead us to the discovery and development of a
whole new way of life, one that has never been possible
before.

In the process of human evolution, we have had to travel
the first two paths. We needed to forget our spiritual origins
long enough to develop our consciousness of physical real-

ity. Then we needed to wake up from the limitation of that reality and remember the spiritual realm. Now the time has come and we are ready to dissolve the split between the two and bring those two realities into one integrated experience.

In order to do this we must strengthen our awareness of our essential roots as spiritual beings. And from that deeply rooted awareness, we must learn to fully embrace our human experience, the reality of our bodies and personalities. Through lovingly embracing the full range of our experience—human and divine—we can heal the split that has existed between spirit and form, in ourselves individually and in the whole world. We can bring the full power and awareness of our spiritual being into our human lives and all our worldly endeavors. Only then will we begin to discover the power and fulfillment that is possible in the physical form. We'll begin to experience what life on earth is really all about!

Of course, this process is already well under way. If you are reading this book, you are most likely already on a transformational path, knowingly or not. If you feel like your life has recently been turned upside down and shaken, then you know for sure that you are!

Following the path of transformation is not necessarily easy. In fact, it can be extremely challenging. Many people at this time are clinging to their material focus, or to their transcendent philosophy, unconsciously hoping they will never have to face the transformational journey. However, if you want to remain in the physical world and continue to evolve, there really is no other choice. In fact, the process is not nearly as arduous as many people fear it will be. While difficult and painful at times, it is also utterly rewarding, exciting, and beautiful.

Rather than rejecting or trying to get beyond all the incredible experiences of our humanness, we can find the beauty and passion in them. We can learn to consciously create our physical reality as an expression of our spiritual being. We can learn to live in the physical world as it was intended to be.

By making a personal commitment to our own individual transformational process, we automatically begin to transform the world around us. As we discover and express more and more of the spiritual potential within us here in our human lives, our personal reality changes to reflect our shifts in consciousness. So the world around us changes as we change. And since we are all linked through the mass consciousness, as we grow we affect everyone else in the world. In choosing to follow the path of transformation, we are not only changing our own lives, we are changing the world.

TWO

ON THE PATH
OF TRANSFORMATION

*So if you really want to help this world,
what you will have to teach is how to
live in it. And that no one can do who
has not himself learned how to live in it
in the joyful sorrow and sorrowful joy of
the knowledge of life as it is.*

— JOSEPH CAMPBELL

FINDING
YOUR INNER TEACHER

Once we've developed a relationship with our own inner teacher and guide, we have access to an unerring source of clarity, wisdom, and direction, right inside us at all times!

How do we follow the path of transformation? One of the first steps is to establish a personal connection with the universal intelligence, or higher power. This higher power exists within everyone and everything. It's the infinitely wise aspect of our being that simply "knows" everything that we need to be aware of at any given time, providing us with guidance from moment to moment, step by step throughout our lives.

There is nothing complicated or mysterious about this higher power. It's a very natural part of our existence. It comes to us through our intuitive sense, our gut feelings. We are all born into this world with this intuitive guidance system. And, if we had all been raised in an enlightened way, we would have learned to follow this inner guidance throughout our lives. Instead, most of us did not receive much support or encouragement in trusting our own deepest feelings. In fact, many of us were actively taught not to trust ourselves but instead to follow an external authority, often in the form of rules or dogma. Or we were encouraged to be rational—to the exclusion of our intuitive faculties.

As adults we can take responsibility for rediscovering and reconnecting with our natural intuitive sense. As we learn to listen to and follow our intuition, we develop an increasingly trusting and powerful relationship with our own inner guidance.

On the path of transformation, it is essential to develop this relationship with our inner guidance because on this path there are no final outside authorities. There are no holy texts or priests, ministers, or gurus who represent the absolute word of God. There is no dogma to follow. Instead, our primary guidance must come from our inner source.

In the Eastern transcendent traditions, and in many of the New Age groups that are modeled after them, there is a belief that one must surrender to an enlightened teacher in order to progress on one's spiritual journey. However, from the perspective of the transformational path, there are no fully enlightened teachers. The traditional masters and gurus are only enlightened in the transcendent sense. They may be able to teach us a great deal about our spiritual development, but they can't show us how to integrate that fully into our human lives on earth, since they have not yet learned to do that themselves.

We are not alone on this new path. There are teachers who can help us with certain aspects of the journey. However, there is no one who has already truly "made it" on this journey because we are all still learning. If anyone was fully integrated, we would all be, since we're all one in the mass consciousness. Rather, we are all moving along the path, more or less together. In a very real way we are each other's teachers and mirrors, reflecting each other's process. Some people are more developed in certain ways and can teach the rest of us what they have learned. However, each person's journey is unique, so ultimately no one but you knows what you need to do.

Do we, then, *need* teachers on the path of transformation? And if so, what is their appropriate role in our lives? How can we relate to them in a way that is healthy and most supportive to our growth?

Yes, I believe that most of us absolutely need teachers on this path. Perhaps there are rare exceptions to this—for example, people who are exceptionally attuned to their own inner knowledge or people who live in very isolated places and learn from nature rather than from human teachers.

Teachers, healers, and guides come in many different forms and often play crucial roles at certain times in our journey. Someone in our lives, for instance, may be the initial catalyst or inspiration that helps us get on a consciousness path. In the earlier stages of our process, almost all of us need information, feedback, support, and guidance of some sort. In a sense, we are in the childhood stage of the consciousness journey and may need a wise parental figure to show us the way. As we gain more knowledge and experience, we gradually develop more trust in ourselves, but we still may need wiser and more experienced people as resources, much as we do when we are adolescents and young adults learning to take our place in the community.

Eventually, once we are mature in our consciousness process, we may be primarily following our own inner direction. Yet the nature of life is constant growth, so at times of stress or crisis, or whenever we are going through a major change, deepening, or expansion of consciousness, we may once again need some outer guidance.

The pitfall in relating to teachers or healers of any kind is the tendency we have to give too much of our power away to them. When we haven't yet fully recognized and owned our inner wisdom, goodness, creativity, and power, we tend to project these qualities onto our mentors and teachers. This is perfectly natural. As we grow, we become aware that these qualities reside in us, and we begin to claim them more and more as our own. A clear and wise teacher helps and supports us in the process of owning our own power. Such a teacher encourages us to take independent steps as soon as we feel we are ready.

Unfortunately, there are many teachers, therapists, and healers who are unclear in this regard. They are overly attached to being in a power position with their students or clients, or to having them remain dependent for too long. This takes care of certain emotional, and often financial, needs on the part of the leader, but it inhibits or severely impairs the growth and empowerment process of the client or student.

I know many people who have suffered greatly from this type of over-attachment to a leader or teacher. In fact, one close friend of mine has spent years trying to heal—both emotionally and physically—after finally breaking away from a teacher who had many fine qualities but unconsciously entrapped her students in dependent relationships with her.

So I must warn readers to beware of teachers, workshop leaders, therapists, healers, or any others who claim to have all the answers (or more than anyone else), who regard themselves as more enlightened or farther along the path than anyone else, or who generally seem to have an inflated sense of themselves. They may be very developed in certain areas, and have much to share, but we need to be cautious and maintain a healthy skepticism in our relationship with them. Proceed with caution if you notice that there seems to be a circle of very dependent devotees who seldom become more empowered in their own lives or move on to other involvements, and who never move into a relationship of more equality and balance with the leader. Also, it may be a danger signal if you feel consistently one-down or inferior to a teacher and he/she seems to cultivate that kind of relationship.

The key to relating to a teacher or healer in a healthy, empowering way is to recognize that person as a mirror of your own inner qualities. If you admire someone for his or her wisdom, love, power, or whatever, recognize that you have those exact qualities within you and that you are drawn to this person as a reflection of the parts of yourself that you need and want to develop. Allow your teacher or therapist to inspire you and show you the way to develop yourself. Afford your teacher respect, admiration, and appreciation, but remind yourself that you are with him or her to learn to love, respect, and honor yourself equally as much! Basically, our teachers are in our lives to help us develop, strengthen, and deepen our relationship to our own inner teacher.

I have had many wonderful teachers, therapists, and guides over the years, each of whom has helped me in a special way. At first, like most people, I put them on pedestals and gave my power away to them. Once or twice I became involved in a very dependent role for awhile. However, each of these experiences was ultimately extremely valuable in helping me to develop my trust in my own inner teacher. Now I have certain people in my life who are teachers and mentors for me, to whom I can turn when I need help, support, and guidance, and with whom I have a relationship of mutual trust, honor, and love.

Because so many of us have been thoroughly conditioned against trusting our inner sources, we simply may not know where to begin the process of developing our relationship with our inner teacher. There are teachers and therapists available in most communities who can help us get on a path of trusting our own inner processes more fully. We recognize these teachers not because they claim to know all the answers but because they are offering skills to help us find those answers ourselves. Even with the best of teachers, however, there comes a time when we may need to let them go, having developed in ourselves the skills we need to trust our own inner guidance.

Once we've developed a relationship with our own inner teacher and guide, we have access to an unerring source of clarity, wisdom, and direction, right inside us at all times! Needless to say, this can be quite comforting, especially in moments of fear and confusion. It gives us the basic sense of trust that we need, in order to have the courage to make this journey. From it we gain the confidence that we are not alone, that there is a higher power guiding our way and helping us along.

Developing
Inner Guidance

Most of us have been trained to automatically deny, ignore, or discount our intuitive feelings to the point where we don't even know we have them. So we need to retrain ourselves to recognize and pay attention to our inner promptings.

How do we go about establishing and developing a relationship with our inner guidance? I've been teaching a process for doing this for many years, and I'm happy to say that most people find it easy to do once they understand the principles and have the opportunity to practice a few simple steps.

One principle to remember is that when we are following our intuitive sense we are following our natural way of living. If doing this seems difficult at first, it is because we have been trained not to do what comes naturally to us. When we pursue these abilities, we are not trying to cultivate super-normal capacities. On the contrary, the process is really one of *un-learning* habits that have prevented us from being able to sense what's true and right for us in our lives.

Most of us have been trained to automatically deny, ignore, or discount our intuitive feelings to the point where we don't even know we have them. So we need to retrain ourselves to recognize and pay attention to our inner promptings.

As you go through the following exercise, remind yourself that we all have intuitive inner guidance. Just because we may not feel it or trust it right now doesn't mean it isn't there. It's always there. What you are doing now is learning to reconnect with it.

Here are some simple steps that can help you contact and cultivate your inner guidance:

1. Relax. If you know a particular relaxation or meditation technique that works for you, such as counting your breaths, saying a mantra, progressive relaxation (often taught in natural childbirth classes), or anything else that allows you to relax your body and quiet your mind, use it. I have included a relaxation exercise in the Appendix of this book for those who would like a program to follow.

In the modern world, we are so accustomed to living in a more or less constant state of stress that we are hardly able to recognize the difference between how it feels to be in a state of tension and how it feels to be relaxed. If you have difficulty with the relaxation exercise I include, you may want to consider taking a class in stress reduction or meditation or using an appropriate audio or video tape.

If you consistently have real difficulty learning to relax, try first doing something enjoyable that requires physical exertion, such as walking or running outdoors, or playing lively music and dancing until you feel tired. Then lie down and relax deeply.

If you have good relaxation skills, choose a time and place where you will not be disturbed by other people, the phone, answering the door, where you will not be reminded of things you need to be doing. Try putting on some soft, soothing music. Sit or lie down comfortably with your spine straight and supported, and take a few minutes to quiet your mind.

2. Once you feel relaxed, allow your awareness to move into a deep place in the core of your body, near your heart or your solar plexus (wherever feels right to you). Affirm that in this place deep inside, you have access to your inner guidance. You can do this with a simple affirmations, such as: "I am moving into the place, deep within me, where I can sense and trust my own inner guidance."

3. Ask a question, such as "What do I need to know (or remember) in my life right now?" or "What direction do I need to take in my life right now?" Or you can ask something more specific, such as, "What do I need to know about my job right now?" or "What do I need to understand about my relationship at this time?"

4. Once you have posed the question, just let it go, and relax quietly, being receptive and open. Notice what thoughts, feelings, or images come to you in response to the question(s) you have asked. If you feel that nothing relevant comes to you, or you feel as confused or uncertain as ever, that's okay, just let it go for now. Guidance doesn't necessarily come immediately in the form of definite ideas or feelings—although it may, especially as you practice and gain more confidence. It often comes later, through a gradually dawning awareness or feeling about the issue. Or it may come through some seemingly external means—like you walk into a bookstore and "just happen" to pick up a book and read a relevant paragraph, or a friend makes a chance remark that strikes a strong chord for you.

5. Once you feel complete with this exercise, just get up and go about your life.

Practice this simple meditation once a day—or at very least twice a week. Most people find that the best times of the day to do this are in the morning upon awakening or before they go to sleep at night. But find what works best for you.

6. Throughout the day, pause and notice your gut feelings about things. Over the next few days, try to notice and be especially aware of your thoughts, feelings, and experiences related to the issue you've asked about. Practice following any intuitive impulses or gut feelings you have, and notice how things work out. You will probably discover that there is a particular quality to your intuitive sense. For example, many people describe it as a sense of "being in the flow" or "being centered," or a feeling of "quiet excitement."

When you are faced with even a simple choice or decision, such as where to eat lunch, whether or not to call a friend, or which movie to see, briefly quiet your mind and go inside. Instead of making your choice on the basis of logical reasoning, or what you think is "correct," or what others might wish, go by what your intuitive guidance tells you.

Pay attention to whatever feedback you get from the way things unfold in your external experience. See how things work out when you follow your own inner guidance. If things don't seem to be working out, it may be because you are not yet fully attuned with your inner guidance. You may be following other feelings instead. The best indication that you are in tune with your inner truth is that you feel more alive as a result. Also, things generally work more easily. Doors open. There's a sense of following a certain flow of energy.

Start with small steps first. Don't make radical moves such as quitting your job, leaving a relationship or spending a large sum of money because you think you have gotten an "intuitive hit" to do that. Start with simple feelings in the moment—this feels right to me or this doesn't. For example, if you are invited to a social event, check in with yourself to see if it feels right before accepting or declining. Live by your inner truth in small, simple ways before you tackle major issues. Seemingly, small steps in this regard may be very significant. As you practice these small steps, you build power and confidence in your connection to your inner guidance.

If you try the six steps I have suggested for awhile and don't feel that you are getting any stronger sense of connection with your inner guidance, here are some further suggestions that may help you:

♦ You are probably trying too hard to make something happen instead of simply allowing it to happen. You may be making the process into a bigger deal than it really is. Relax and let go. Stop trying to make anything amazing happen. Just listen a little more deeply than usual for your own sense of truth.

♦ If you feel a lot of confusion and inner conflict, and can't distinguish your intuitive sense from all your other thoughts and feelings, try to identify some of the different voices inside you. Take different color pens and write out what each of them has to say.

For example, if you are trying to figure out whether to change a particular course you have been following in your life—in your career, a hobby, a relationship—you might discover that there is a very fearful voice. Try using a black pen to thoroughly write out what this voice is saying: i.e., "Don't try anything new, it might be a disaster!" You might discover that you have a conservative voice that tells you, "Maybe you'd better stay with what's familiar." You could use a blue pen to write what this voice is saying. You might get in touch with a creative voice that tells you, "I have a wonderful idea for starting a new business!" whose thoughts you might like to record with a green pen. Then again, you may find that you have a risk-taking voice that says, "Go ahead, do something new and exciting!" Record what it has to say with a red pen.

You may, of course, have other voices that I have not mentioned here—a playful child voice, a mischievous one, a voice that is aloof or skeptical. You may become aware of a voice that sounds like one of your parents, your spouse, your boss, or someone else you know or have known. Whatever comes up for you, take the time to write down everything it says, using whatever colored pen or pencil best fits. After you've done this, just let it go for awhile.

♦ Try not to get caught up in needing to have an immediate answer. Life is an ongoing, unfolding process, and you may not be ready yet for a decision or a definite direction. You may be "in process." Inner guidance seldom gives us long-term information; it usually just lets us know what we need in the moment. Sometimes, inner guidance may be saying, "Just wait, don't do anything, allow yourself to be in confusion." When clarity is meant to come, it will. That is the nature of inner guidance.

♦ If you feel really blocked for a long period of time, you probably need to do some emotional healing work. When we are holding our emotions inside us, it can be difficult or even impossible to contact our intuitive feelings. If you feel you may be having difficulties of this kind, find a good therapist or support group and begin the process of learning to experience and express your emotions. Once you've done a certain amount of deep emotional healing, you will automatically be more in touch with your intuition.

♦ If you are following what you think are your intuitive feelings, but you aren't feeling more enlivened and aware, and your life doesn't seem to be in motion, then you probably are confusing your intuitive feelings with other emotions or impulses. You may need some help clarifying what's what.

Also, it's very important to learn to distinguish intuitive feelings and impulses from addictive ones. If I have a drinking problem or an eating disorder, and I have a sudden strong impulse to have a drink or eat an ice cream sundae, that is not my intuitive guidance. If I'm a workaholic and I have a deep feeling that I need to go into the office on Sunday despite my family's objections, I probably need to question where that impulse is coming from. Our intuitive guidance is always trying to help us in the direction of bringing balance and real fulfillment into our lives. In order to hear it clearly, we have to be able to recognize our addictive tendencies and learn not to be controlled by them. If you sense that you may have an active addiction, seek help from a twelve-step program or therapist specializing in addiction.

♦ And finally, remember that developing inner guidance is a lifelong, ever-deepening process. I've been working on it for years, and I'm still learning and developing my ability to sense and trust my inner truth. Like all things in life, the process goes in cycles. Sometimes, my inner guidance is coming through clear and strong, and I feel completely in the flow of life. At other times I feel confused and lost, uncertain why things are happening the way they are and not knowing what to do about them. I've learned to trust those times, too, and know that eventually I come out the other side with greater awareness. A friend of mine calls this "the lull," which is as natural a part of our lives as the normal pause between heartbeats or between the exhalation and inhalation of breath.*

Inner guidance is always there inside us, and it is always correct, wise, and loving. We may lose touch with it, or misinterpret it at times. We may try to push too hard and get ahead of ourselves. But our inner teacher never abandons us. We are never alone.

---

* My book, *Living in the Light,* has many exercises to help you develop your ability to follow your intuitive guidance. Or you may find my tape, *Developing Intuition,* helpful.

THE FOUR LEVELS
OF EXISTENCE

All four levels of being are closely related to and affected by one another. As we heal one level, we support the healing process of all the other levels as well.

Human life consists of four levels of being — spiritual, mental, emotional, and physical. The path of transformation involves clearing, healing, developing, and integrating all four of these levels.

All of these levels are equally important. There isn't one that we can skip or neglect if we want to experience wholeness. We need to focus time and attention on healing and developing each one. As we do this, all four levels naturally begin to balance and become more fully integrated with one another.

We may begin our consciousness journey at any of these levels. It's different for each person. For example, many people get involved in a consciousness process because they have a physical crisis — a disease, an accident, a weight issue or an addiction problem. Or they simply develop an interest in living a healthier lifestyle; they start learning more about nutrition and exercise, one thing leads to another, and eventually they are discovering all kinds of new ideas and ways of living that take them beyond the physical level.

For other people it may be an emotional crisis or need that brings them into the journey. Perhaps someone seeks counseling for grief over the loss of a loved one, and begins to discover much more about themselves that they want to explore even further. Or because of an addiction problem, they join a twelve-step program (Alcoholics Anonymous, Narcotics Anonymous, etc.) which brings them into a consciousness journey.

Still others may enter the process on the mental level. Motivated initially by intellectual curiosity they begin by reading philosophy, psychology, or consciousness books. I have heard many stories about people who by chance picked up a particular book, read a chapter and whose life was never quite the same again.

So there are many different ways the process may get started. Once we have begun, we may move from one level to another at different times, or we may work on two, three, or all four levels simultaneously. Each person's path is unique.

Generally, however, no matter where we start our consciousness journey, or how we proceed with it, there's a certain underlying evolutionary process that unfolds from the spiritual to the physical.

Somewhere along the line, we have a profound spiritual experience. Such an event may appear to happen by chance, before we even know there is a conscious path to follow. In fact, that event may be the catalyst precipitating a crisis which, in turn, leads to the beginning of our conscious journey. Or it may happen later, after we are already conscious seekers. In any case, whenever it happens, it changes our life forever. It gives us a glimpse of a higher perspective on life, and a taste of the feelings of love, power, and bliss that are possible to experience.

I remember meeting a woman in her middle forties who had been faced with cancer twelve years before. During an operation, she had a near-death experience, in which she saw herself bathed in white light that was helping in her healing. When the operation was over, she kept having recurring visions of the light. At the same time that she was bathed in this light she was filled with feelings of complete and total peace and oneness.

Prior to this time she had never considered herself to be a spiritual or religious person. But over the next few months she began to pursue that path, one she has been on ever since. She said that what happened to her in surgery opened her eyes to a very different level of reality than she had ever before recognized.

This is a fairly dramatic example of a life-changing spiritual experience. For many of us it may take a more subtle or gradual form. But the eventual result is the same.

Having had these experiences, we can no longer be content with a limited way of living; we are compelled to seek greater awareness. We try to understand what happened to us so that we can repeat and/or expand the experience. This leads to experimentation with spiritual practices, and exploration on the mental level as we let go of old ideas and open up to new ones. Eventually, usually after a few years of work on the spiritual and mental levels, we find ourselves increasingly bumping into the emotional level of our being. For many of us, the emotional level can feel like a wall, seeming to prevent us from fully living our spiritual beliefs in our daily lives.

It seems that what's keeping us from living our new philosophies is our old emotional patterns. For example, we may have had moments of spiritual clarity or breakthrough in which we really felt that there is a higher power taking care of us. We may understand that idea intellectually and be committed to living our lives accordingly, trusting our inner guidance to show us what we need to know. Yet we may repeatedly find ourselves wrestling with feelings of fear and terror, unable to let go of our old ways of controlling our lives.

This is a perfectly natural part of the process. Just because we've experienced something at the spiritual level, and we now understand it mentally, we haven't necessarily integrated it at the emotional level. To heal and transform ourselves at the emotional level of our being demands a whole different focus, requiring time, patience, and compassion for ourselves. And, it usually requires a lot of help from other people as well.

Once we have done a substantial amount of work on the spiritual, mental, and emotional levels, we have the great challenge of bringing it all into the physical level. Here we have the opportunity to actually bring everything we have been learning and discovering into our daily lives, living fully and freely, moment by moment. This often requires some healing of the body itself.

In the next four chapters, I will explain a little more about these levels and how the healing/transformational process takes place on each one of them.

All four levels of being are closely related to and affected by one another. As we heal one level, we support the healing process of all the other levels as well. Strengthening our spiritual connection gives us the inspiration and strength to face deep emotional healing, for example. As we do our emotional healing work, we release blocked energies on the mental and physical levels as well. And the more in tune we are with our physical bodies, the more energy we feel on every level. We may begin the process on any level and explore the various realms at different times in our lives. The ultimate goal is the integration of them all.

Healing
the Spiritual Level

Spiritual healing occurs as we begin to consciously reconnect with our essential being—the wise, loving, powerful, creative entity that we are at our core. Through this connection with our spiritual essence . . . we experience a sense of safety, trust, and fulfillment, a feeling of belonging in the universe.

Most of us who have grown up in the modern world have experienced a profound disconnection from our spiritual selves and from the universal source. This causes an underlying feeling of emptiness, insecurity, and meaninglessness in our lives. Unconsciously we seek to fill this inner void in many fruitless ways. We may strive for money, power, and success as a way of feeling secure, or we may devote ourselves to our families or careers as a way of finding meaning and purpose. We may succumb to various addictive behaviors, using food, drugs, work, or sex to try to fill the empty feeling. Unfortunately, none of these efforts reaches the underlying problem.

The lack of spiritual connection in our culture is at the root of many of our social as well as personal ills. The epidemic use of drugs by our young people, as well as the proliferation of gangs in our inner cities, have their roots in the deepest levels of spiritual alienation and need. The development of bizarre religious cults is also symptomatic of the search for meaning and authentic spiritual experience. When we live in or visit areas that have been particularly hard hit by the recent breakdown of our socioeconomic systems, we encounter much depression and rage—which comes about when people have no spiritual or psychological base for dealing with the pressures they are facing.

Spiritual healing occurs as we begin to consciously reconnect with our essential being—the wise, loving, powerful, creative entity that we are at our core. Through this connection with our spiritual essence, we begin to reexperience our oneness with all other beings and with all of nature. The more we connect with this essential oneness, the more we experience a sense of safety, trust, and fulfillment, a feeling of belonging in the universe. We experience our inner emptiness being filled by the spirit within.

This contact with our spiritual self gives us an expanded perspective on our lives, both as individuals and as part of humanity. Rather than just being caught up in the daily frustrations and struggles of our personality, we are able to see things from the perspective of the soul. We're able to look at the bigger picture of life on earth, which helps us to understand a lot more about why we're here and what we're doing. It helps to make our daily problems seem not quite so huge, and makes our lives feel more meaningful.

For example, the island of Kauai, where I live, was recently struck by a powerful hurricane. The island was devastated. Few died, but thousands of buildings were destroyed or, like my home, severely damaged. There were shortages of water, food, power, and shelter. Many lost not only their homes but all their possessions, their businesses, and their jobs. It was a frightening and stressful time.

Yet, for those with a spiritual perspective, it was clearly a transformational event. Almost everyone going through it reconnected with their deepest values and priorities—the sense that life, family, and community are so much more important than physical possessions. Many people were forced to get clear about changes they needed to make, or new steps they needed to take in their lives. While the experience brought pain and suffering to many, it has also brought tremendous healing for those who are able to see it that way.

The spiritual level gives us a foundation from which we can more easily move into other levels of healing. Without at least starting our spiritual healing it may be very difficult, or even impossible, to find the hope, understanding, and strength we need to confront the difficulties and challenges of healing the other levels.

Spiritual healing begins when we find a way to make regular contact with the spiritual aspect of ourselves. This means developing a spiritual practice that works for us, and then making a commitment to doing it on a regular basis, daily or at least weekly. For some people this might be silent meditation, alone or in a group; it might be attending church services or some other type of group inspirational activity. For others it might take place through regular contact with nature—walks in the woods, hikes in the mountains, sitting quietly near a river or the ocean.

A spiritual practice need not be religious in the usual sense. Many people find their spiritual connection primarily through physical activity—walking, running, dancing, bicycling. Others find it through a creative activity such as painting or making music. Some find it in serving others, and some find it in quiet moments with family and loved ones. A friend of mine takes a day of silence each week. All his close friends know this is his day of rest—to rest his voice, his mind, and his body and listen keenly to his internal guidance. If a full day is not possible for you, start with an hour or two in the late afternoon or evening, when you will simply be alone, with a quiet mind and no outside distractions—no phone, no television, no visitors.

For many people, Sunday is a good day to honor our spiritual needs since this is a day which our society has actually set aside for spiritual or religious nurturing. One of my friends doesn't have any organized religious affiliations but she keeps her time open on Sundays to listen to what she alone needs, freeing herself from obligation and plans. In this way she renews her inner self, and makes ready for a busy schedule during the coming week.

Whatever works for you is great . . . just make certain that you have some form of spiritual inspiration and renewal as a regular part of your life.

The steps described in the chapter on developing inner guidance provide one form of spiritual practice. Our inner guidance comes from the spiritual center within us, so as we learn to trust and follow our intuition, we are building a strong relationship with our spiritual being.

MEDITATION

Tuning Into Your Spiritual Being

Meditation is a way of taking time to become aware of our thoughts, feelings, and bodily sensations, then allowing ourselves to drop into a deeper level of being. Here is a simple exercise that can help you begin your spiritual practice.

Find a spot to designate as your place of spiritual retreat, somewhere close to home or work so that you can have regular, easy access to it. It's wonderful if this place can be outdoors, with some natural beauty around it. Most importantly, though, it should be quiet, peaceful, and comfortable. It could be a spot in your back yard, a special room in your house, or a corner of a room.

Make it special by designating a certain chair, pillow, and/or blanket that you only use while meditating. Make sure you will be uninterrupted for at least fifteen minutes, or longer if possible.

Find a comfortable position either sitting or lying down. Make sure it's a position where your body can completely relax.

Take a deep breath, slowly, filling your lungs. Then, as you exhale, again slowly and easily, let your body relax. Take another deep breath and as you exhale, relax your body a little more. With every breath, as you exhale, relax your body a little more deeply.

As you continue to breathe deeply and slowly, notice how you are feeling emotionally. Don't try to analyze why you are feeling that way, and don't try to change how you are feeling. Simply acknowledge and accept how you are feeling. For example, "I notice that I'm feeling a little depressed right now," or "I'm aware that I'm feeling anxious, remembering all the work I have to do," or "I'm feeling calm and peaceful at the moment." Allow the feeling(s) to just be there. You need do nothing about them except to accept them.

Notice the thoughts that are going through your mind. Watch them for awhile as they parade across your mind, like one of those electronic billboards: "Well, here I am trying to watch my thoughts. Let's see, what am I thinking? This reminds me of the time I went to that meditation retreat . . . There was that weird guy there. He reminded me of . . . whoops, I'm supposed to be watching my thoughts." Imagine your mind slowing down and going slightly out of focus. Thoughts will continue to arise, but don't hold onto them. As soon as you notice you are having a thought, let it go.

Continue to breathe deeply and slowly as you relax your body, accept your feelings, and allow your mind to slow down a little.

Now, imagine moving your awareness deeper inside, deeper and deeper into the core of your being, deeper than your body, your mind, or your emotions. Allow yourself to sit quietly and just be with yourself in a deep place inside. Know that this is the place where you can contact your spiritual being.

Ask to be in touch with the part of you that is deeper than your body, mind, and emotions. Sit quietly. Continue to notice any thoughts, feelings, or images that come to you. Notice and accept anything that happens within you. If you wish, ask for guidance or inspiration, or whatever you feel you need. Accept whatever comes, or doesn't come, without analyzing it.

After you've been there quietly for fifteen minutes (or as long as you wish), give thanks to your spiritual being. Then get up slowly and gently, and go about your life.

Sometimes when you do this, you may feel that nothing happens. Or you may find at times that you obsess about certain thoughts or feelings and can't really relax. This is normal and natural. As you practice this meditation regularly for awhile, you will probably find it gets easier to drop into a relaxed, quiet state of mind. If not, then take a class in meditation or relaxation techniques, or try a different method of spiritual practice.

Some of the practices that people find helpful, either for learning to relax so they can meditate, or instead of meditating are: progressive relaxation; counting your breaths (sitting with eyes closed and counting each breath —in 1, out 2, in 3, out 4, etc.); dancing to your favorite music until you sweat; sitting quietly while focusing on an object such as a flower, the flame of a candle, a sound; chanting, drumming, or listening to music which is calming and repetitive.*

---

* Many simple and powerful meditations and spiritual practices can be found in the book *Coming Home: The Return to True Self*, by Martia Nelson.

HEALING
THE MENTAL LEVEL

To experience balance, integration, and well-being, our belief systems and thought processes need to support and be in harmony with the other three levels of our existence—the physical, emotional, and spiritual.

The mental level of our being is our intellect, that is, the rational mind. In order to clear and heal the mental level, we need to become conscious of our thoughts and underlying belief systems. We need to educate ourselves about other ideas and beliefs, and eventually be able to consciously choose the ideas that make most sense to us and make our lives work the best.

We've all learned certain viewpoints and attitudes about the world through the early influences of our families, religions, schools, and our culture as a whole. For example, around the time of Columbus, most people believed the world was flat, and if you sailed far enough out to sea you'd fall off the edge of the earth. People held that picture of the earth in their minds and saw it as the truth because that was what their parents, teachers, and society believed and taught. When explorers like Christopher Columbus successfully challenged these beliefs, however, it created a whole new inner vision of the world in our minds.

There's a wonderful teaching story told by Deepak Chopra that further makes this point. When training baby elephants in India, trainers start by chaining one hind leg of the animal to a large tree. In a short time the elephant becomes so accustomed to the chain that he no longer tries to free himself. The trainers then reduce the size of the chain. In time, the elephant is so conditioned to the restraint that even a tiny cord around that foot will stop him. Yet it is certainly not the cord that holds him; rather, it is his belief that he is restrained.

Like the elephant, our belief systems color our experience of the world, and we tend to keep interpreting our experiences and recreating our world based on our core beliefs about ourselves, other people, life. However, as we mature and have new and different experiences of life, new ideas and perspectives may challenge our beliefs. Every moment of our lives we are involved in an ongoing process of sorting out and evolving our philosophy of life.

To experience balance, integration, and well-being, our belief systems and thought processes need to support and be in harmony with the other three levels of our existence, the physical, emotional, and spiritual. We need to have a spiritual understanding, or life philosophy, that helps us find meaning in our lives. We need to have an understanding and acceptance of our own emotions that help us to accept ourselves. And we need to know how to care for our physical bodies in a healthy way.

If you have a belief that your physical body is inferior to your spiritual self, for example, and that it is unworthy of your care or attention, you are holding onto a mental attitude that will cause conflict and lack of well-being in your system. But if you were to reeducate yourself to understand how important and worthy your physical body is, and you learned to take good care of it, you would find more balance and harmony in your entire system.

In the process of becoming more conscious, we are constantly learning new ideas, viewpoints and philosophies, and weighing them against the ones we already hold. Gradually, we begin letting go of the old ideas that are too limiting for us, while retaining the ones that still serve us and incorporating new ones that are more expansive, deepening, and empowering.

For example, I used to believe that there wasn't much I could do about the circumstances of my life, that I didn't have much power to change them. Then I learned the idea that I create my own reality. I found that idea much more empowering, so I eventually chose to adopt that belief system. As I did this, I began to experience the world in a very different way and began to see that I really could have a great deal of power over the circumstances of my life.

I had grown up believing that I would choose a life career and go to college for many years in order to achieve my goals. But after four years of college I still didn't know exactly what I wanted to do! I discovered a new philosophy, that by trusting and following my intuitive guidance and creative impulses, my life would develop in interesting and fulfilling ways. A fascinating and successful career has unfolded from following this belief system—and I never went back to college!

Many people are confused about the process of healing the mental level. They think they must always practice "positive thinking," using that technique to block out their negative thoughts. They're afraid their negative thoughts will hurt them. Perhaps they have been stuck in negative thoughts and feelings at one time in their lives. Now that they are feeling more positive, they don't want to acknowledge *any* negatives for fear of "slipping back" into a negative perspective. So they deny or repress all their negative thoughts and concentrate only on the positive ones. For some people this works fairly well for awhile, but eventually all those denied or repressed thoughts and feelings have to come to the surface, one way or another. That is why many people who attempt to practice positive thinking are quite surprised to discover that efforts to get rid of their negative thinking actually makes matters worse. Rather than diminishing their negative thoughts and feelings, they find themselves caught up in them even more.

Remember that the first step in any healing process is always acknowledgement and acceptance of what is true right now. We don't heal anything by trying to block it out, get rid of it, or pretend it doesn't exist. We heal it by accepting that it's there, and then becoming aware that there are other choices possible. So we need to acknowledge and accept our "negative" thoughts as part of who we are, and at the same time recognize and develop other perspectives and ideas that give us more expansive possibilities.

For example, Susan recognizes that there's a part of her that says she's not worthy or deserving of happiness. She notices herself sometimes getting stuck in these self-critical thoughts. Whenever she makes a mistake, her inner critic says, "You see, this is just further proof that you can't do anything right."

Susan can't change this by simply censoring herself every time her inner critic speaks up. Rather, she needs to acknowledge those thoughts, and perhaps delve a little more deeply into them. One question she might ask herself is: "Where did these thoughts come from, anyway?" Upon reflection, she realizes that the voice in her head is very similar to her mother's voice, who used to criticize her just as she now criticizes herself.

With this awareness, she can begin seeking tools for learning to heal and transform her inner critic.* If she had

---

* There is an excellent and most helpful book on this topic by Drs. Hal and Sidra Stone, *Embracing Your Inner Critic.*

simply tried to block out her negative thoughts, she would have lost the opportunity to learn from them, and she might have spent the rest of her life struggling to repress her negative thoughts instead of finding a way to truly heal them.

Some people have had the childhood experience of being told they were stupid, or they had their abilities compared unfavorably with a sibling or classmate. Many girls were given the message, directly or indirectly, that females are less intelligent, or that they are less important than males. And many people with more intuitive, holistic, right-brain learning styles were never supported by our left-brain, logically oriented society and school system; as a result, many may have drawn the mistaken conclusion that they are less intelligent than others.

People who have suffered these types of traumas in early life may have learned to doubt, discount, or deny their own intellect. In this case, the mental healing process must involve reclaiming one's own natural intelligence and learning to trust it. Remember that there are many different kinds of intelligence. Our culture tends to validate only certain types of abilities. An acquaintance of mine is not very educated or articulate, but he is brilliant at fixing mechanical things and finds great joy in his work.

Similarly, I met a woman some years ago who was an excellent baker. She had a low I.Q. as measured by standard tests but was very talented in her chosen profession, and very interesting, open, and loving. I always felt she made a tremendous contribution in that she brought a real light into any room she entered. I think of her as an example of a truly happy person, delighted with life and delightful to be around.

Our society tends to reward only one kind of intelligence — book learning. But there are actually many different kinds of intelligence. In his book, *Raising a Magical Child*, Joseph Chilton Pearce talks about the seven intelligences:*

---

* Published by Dutton, New York, 1992

Physical intelligence

Emotional intelligence

Intellectual intelligence

Social intelligence

Conceptual intelligence

Intuitive intelligence

Imaginative intelligence

To this list we could add many others, such as:

Spiritual intelligence

Musical intelligence

"Tracking" (wilderness) intelligence

"Street smarts"

Similarly, some people are more oriented to what has come to be called "right brain" abilities, that is, the more artistic, non-linear, less structured activities. Others are more oriented to "left brain" abilities, structured, linear processes such as mathematics, verbal and technical skills.

Certainly, each type of intelligence has its own niche. For example, if you were lost in a jungle you'd obviously be much better off with a guide who had "tracking" intelligence than you would with a person who was a great academic! And if your car broke down fifty miles from the nearest town, the person with physical intelligence (which includes the mechanical), is probably going to be a lot more helpful than the one with intellectual intelligence.

In each kind of intelligence is a clue to the gift we have come here to give. Every one of us has our own gift, from the agile rock climber to the "fix-it genius," to the single mother who raises three healthy kids and maintains a full-time job. It is ironic but very true that we are often the last ones in the world to be able to see and acknowledge our own gifts or areas of intelligence. Most of us are pretty blind to the things we do best. While low self-esteem can contribute to this blindness, a bigger factor is that we live with our genius every day and it just seems "normal" to us.

When I was a kid, I read and wrote constantly. The library was my favorite place and I used to imagine a whole shelf full of books that I had written! This was, and is, one of my areas of intelligence and it is a course I have recognized and been able to follow through most of my life. However, it is not always easy to immediately recognize our gifts.

For example, my editor, Hal Bennett, tells how in his childhood he loved reading and writing but was discouraged by his inability to diagram sentences and remember rules of grammar, which were required in the schools he attended. Eventually he became convinced that he was, in his words, "just plain stupid where school was concerned," and he virtually gave up trying. He graduated from high school only by taking special summer classes, and his family never expected him to go any further with his schooling.

When he was twenty-one, he enrolled in a night school class in creative writing which completely changed the course of his life. He wrote a short story which the class loved and which later was published in a literary magazine. That was the encouragement he needed to pursue his gift and his unique intelligence. Since the days of that creative writing class he has gone on to get university degrees in writing, holistic health and a doctorate in psychology. He has published twelve books of his own, another twenty as a co-author. But what he best loves is working with other writers to help them develop and refine their own work.

The path he followed in his life was to pursue his early interests even though he felt discouraged and had many mixed messages around what he could and couldn't do. A similar path can be helpful for anyone who has somehow been discouraged from pursuing their own gifts and early interests.

EXERCISE

Rediscovering Your Native Intelligence

Think about the various kinds of intelligences I listed in the paragraphs above—or any other kinds of intelligence you may have observed on your own. What kinds of intelligence do you have? You may actually have a unique combination of several of the intelligences noted above, plus one or more others that you may have thought of.

To help you open your eyes to your own intelligence, remember back to the activities you gravitated toward as a kid. Exploring nature? Reading? Making up stories? Playing with animals? Putting on plays? Taking things apart to see how they work? Sports? Music? Others?

Take a moment to write down a list of things you do well or that you really like to do. Is there a common thread that runs through them? Follow the thread. It will lead you to your own unique intelligence.

As you get in touch with your own intelligence, you may also recognize that you were rewarded, discouraged, belittled, or encouraged in the area of your greatest interest. If you had negative experiences where your intelligence is concerned, start reaffirming your abilities right now by recognizing that your natural gift and unique intelligence are found in those activities and interests toward which you were drawn in your early life. There is a reason you gravitated in that direction, and the inner compass that pointed that particular direction is rarely, if ever, wrong.

If you need to do some healing around your gift, look for ways that you might start today to develop those early interests. Pursue skills and knowledge in that area through taking classes, or by getting to know other people who have successful careers in your field of interest, by reading more about it, and—perhaps most important of all—by doing it for yourself, starting right now.

You begin "doing it" with the faith that your early interests are trustworthy indicators, revealing your true gift. Then you start giving yourself time to focus more of your attention on those early interests. Find some way to get "hands-on" experience: If your early interest is writing, start a writing journal or take a writing class. If you are interested in mechanical things, get a broken down machine of a kind that intrigues you and take it apart. If working with people is your passion, sign up for volunteer work at an agency that helps people. These firsthand involvements not only revive and reaffirm your interests and your "native intelligence," they also get you on your way to actualizing those most important parts of yourself that may have been lost.

HEALING
THE EMOTIONAL LEVEL

Our feelings are an important part of the life force that is constantly moving through us. If we don't allow ourselves to fully experience our emotions, we stop the natural flow of that life force.

For most of us, exploring the spiritual realm is primarily a pleasant, expansive experience. And because we are such a mental culture we are fairly comfortable with the mental aspect of our journey. However, a great many people are stuck at the level where emotional healing needs to take place. Most people are frightened at the prospect of doing deep emotional healing work.

We live in a society that's generally terrified of emotions. Our patriarchal mentality is highly suspicious of the feminine aspect of our being—the feeling, intuitive part of us. The rational side of us is trying to ensure our safety in the physical world, and fears the loss of control that deep emotion brings. Since our culture admires the more male, rational approach to life, and disrespects the more feminine, feeling side, we have all learned, to one degree or another, to hide and deny our feelings—even from ourselves. We've learned to bury most of our feelings deep inside, and show the world only what seems safe, which usually isn't very much.

Most of us are particularly uncomfortable with what are commonly considered "negative" feelings, such as fear, hurt, sadness, grief, and anger. In reality, there is no such thing as a negative feeling. We call things negative because we don't understand them and therefore we fear them. All of these feelings are natural and important. They each serve a meaningful function in the human experience. Rather than rejecting and avoiding them, we need to explore and discover the gift each one offers us. And we need to understand that to fully feel anything, we have to be comfortable feeling the fullness of its opposite. For example, in order to feel real joy, we must be able to embrace our sadness. In order to open to love, we need to accept our fear as part of our experience. Interestingly enough, we are often just as afraid of too much "positive" feeling as we are of the so-called "negative" ones. We don't want to feel too much love, joy, or passion. We prefer the cool middle ground where we can feel in control.

While most of us have learned to repress our feelings, some people have the opposite problem; they are too easily overwhelmed by their emotions and have difficulty maintaining any emotional equilibrium. They are often carrying the repressed emotions of other people around them, feeling and expressing everyone else's feelings as well as their own. Still others are stuck in one particular emotion and are constantly reacting from that place—anger perhaps, or fear. These are all symptoms of emotional imbalances that need healing.

Due at least in part to our fear of feeling, there is a great deal of ignorance and misinformation about healing the emotional level. In fact, many people don't even acknowledge that emotions exist! How many times have you read or heard reference to the *three* levels of existence—body, mind, and spirit? The emotional level is not even acknowledged, but is simply lumped into the mind category. This comes from the traditional transcendent approach, where the importance of the human experience is minimized, and emotions, so much a part of that human experience, are dismissed as fabrications of the mind.

Many teachers and healers confuse the mental and emotional levels, or treat them as one. For example, you may have heard or read a discussion of how our thoughts affect our physical health, with no reference whatsoever of how our feelings affect our physical health. Yet in my experience, blocked emotions are one of the main cause of most physical ailments.

Of course, our mental and emotional energies are quite intertwined, as are all levels of our being. It's not possible to completely separate any of them from the others. But thoughts and feelings, while certainly connected and strongly influencing each other, are very different. Part of healing the emotional level is learning to distinguish between thinking and feeling. In beginning workshops, for example, when a person is asked how they *feel* about, let's say, their boss firing them unexpectedly, the reply may be, "Well, he had no grounds for doing that. I always did my work and then some!" That is a thinking response. A feeling response would be, "I'm angry! And I'm scared."

Our thoughts are much more connected to our conscious mind and our will, whereas our feelings come from a deeper, less rational place. To some degree we can consciously choose our thoughts, but the only choice we have about our feelings is how we handle them. For instance, the person who got fired might choose to indulge himself in critical or vengeful thoughts about his boss, or he might choose to focus on thoughts about how to get another job. However, the underlying emotions of anger and fear are there, regardless. He can choose how he handles those feelings by either sitting at home feeling depressed, going to the office and yelling at the boss, or talking his feelings out with a friend or a therapist, then going job-hunting. In other words, he can repress his feelings, act them out, or explore, express, accept them, and then find appropriate actions to take care of himself.

It's sometimes rather shocking to discover how few people seem to understand the process of emotional healing — even many therapists and healers who are supposedly helping people with that process. Many professionals who are able to help people up to a certain point don't know how to guide them through the deeper levels of emotional healing. This is partly because, in order to guide others successfully we need to have done our own deep healing work, and many therapists have done little if any of this. Fortunately all this is slowly changing; more is being learned every day about emotional healing, and more people are having the courage to go through it. I certainly don't consider myself an expert by any means, but I have learned a good deal from several excellent teachers I've worked with, from going through my own deep emotional healing process and from guiding many others through theirs.

When we were infants and children, we had many strong feelings. What we needed was to have people acknowledge and respond to these feelings in appropriate ways. For example, we needed to hear things like this: "I understand that you're really upset that your brother got to go and you didn't." Or, "I can see that you're feeling really sad about grandpa being sick."

In essence, as children we need validation of our feelings from our parents, families, teachers, and the surrounding world. We need to be assured that we have a right to our feelings, that our feelings aren't wrong or bad. We need to feel that others can understand and empathize with us when we are experiencing strong feelings. In short, we need to be allowed to have our own feeling experience.

Having our feelings validated is, of course, quite different from being allowed to do whatever we want. Children need to be given clear limits and boundaries just as much as they need to be assured that having feelings is okay. Thus, at the same time that a parent might be telling the child, "You can't go out and play now," she could acknowledge that child's feelings, "I know you are disappointed about that. I understand that you're upset because you want to ride your bike right now!"

Because our parents and families were not supported in their own emotional experience as children, most of them did not know how to do that for us. More often than not, they gave us messages that told us that our feelings were wrong, bad, inappropriate or intolerable, such as: "There's no reason to feel that way." Or, "Cheer up! Things aren't so bad!" Or, the classic, "Big boys (or girls) don't cry." Or even worse, "I'll give you something to cry about!" As a result, most of us learned to bury our feelings and present what was considered appropriate.

Even as parents, we may find ourselves treating our own children in ways that we were treated. We tend to pass on the same attitudes and patterns that our parents taught us. If we never healed the belief our parents taught us, for example, that anger or fear is an "unacceptable" feeling, we will tend to pass that lesson on to our own children. And they, in turn, will have the same confusion about their feelings that we have about our own.

No matter how hard parents try, and they all do the best they are capable of, children inevitably experience some degree of emotional hurt, neglect, and abandonment. Because we are so vulnerable as children, we are deeply wounded by these experiences, and we carry our wounds inside us for the rest of our lives—or until we do our conscious emotional healing work.

In emotional healing work we learn to give ourselves, and allow ourselves to receive from others, whatever we didn't receive as young children. We learn to accept and experience all our feelings and, when appropriate, to communicate these feelings in a way that allows others to understand us. We open the way to our emotional healing through the experience of having at least one other person hear, understand, and empathize with what we are feeling.

If we have denied or stuffed down a lot of our feelings, we may need to have a safe place and experienced guide to help us begin to get in touch with, experience, and release them. Then we need to develop tools for staying current with our feelings by allowing ourselves to acknowledge and experience them as they arise. It is important to get in touch with the needs underneath our feelings and learn how to communicate those needs effectively. Underneath most of our emotions are our basic needs for love, acceptance, security, and self-esteem. We need to know the vulnerable child who still lives deep inside each of us, and learn to become the loving parent our own inner child requires.

If we want to experience the full range of our being in this lifetime, we need to commit ourselves to heal the emotional wounds from our childhood and early life. This deep level of emotional healing takes time. It cannot be rushed or forced. It needs to unfold in its own time, sometimes taking a number of years to move through the deeper levels. Fortunately, as each layer is healed, life becomes more and more fulfilling and rewarding.

Our feelings are an important part of the life force that is constantly moving through us. If we don't allow ourselves to fully experience our emotions, we stop the natural flow of that life force. Energy gets blocked in our physical bodies and may remain that way for years or even a lifetime, unless it is released. This leads to emotional and physical pain and disease. Repressed feelings = blocked energy = emotional and physical ailments.

Accepting our emotions, allowing ourselves to feel them, and learning to communicate them constructively and appropriately, allows them to move through us easily and naturally. This enables the full free flow of the life force through our physical bodies, which brings emotional and physical healing. Experiencing feelings = free flowing energy = emotional and physical health and well-being.

I like to use the analogy that our emotions are like the weather, constantly changing—sometimes dark, sometimes light, at times wild and intense, at other times calm and quiet. Trying to resist or control your feeling experience is like trying to control the weather—an exercise in futility and frustration! Besides, if all we ever experienced were sunny days of exactly 75-degree temperature, life might become quite boring. When we can appreciate the beauty of the rain, the wind, and the snow, as well as the sun, we are free to enjoy the fullness of life.

EXERCISE

Healing the Emotional Level

If you become aware of having lost your feeling of well-being during the day, try this simple exercise:

Lie or sit down in a comfortable position and focus your attention, for a moment, on the area of your discomfort, remembering that emotions are held in the body as tension, pain, or other expressions of uneasiness. Usually, you will experience this discomfort somewhere in your torso. Let your attention rest near this discomfort in a caring and soothing way. Let yourself feel the quality of the sensations in that area. When you find your attention drifting, perhaps wondering what could have caused you to have this discomfort, refocus and bring your awareness back to the sensations in your torso. Give permission to your intuitive guidance to bring forth any issues concerning these feelings. You can do this simply by asking, "Is there something you want me to know?" Then be careful that you don't abandon the area of feeling. Allow yourself to receive a sense of what is going on there. Even if you don't ever get a message, just attending to the area in this way, allowing yourself to feel it, will encourage any blocked energy to move more easily through it.

Also, the book, *Passion to Heal: The Ultimate Guide to Your Healing Journey*, by Echo Bodine, has many excellent exercises for deep emotional healing. It is listed in the Recommended Resources section at the end of this book.

HEALING
THE PHYSICAL LEVEL

The overall process of physical healing takes place in our lives as we learn to feel, listen to, and trust our bodies again. Our bodies . . . communicate to us clearly and specifically, if we are willing to listen to them.

Since the spiritual, mental, and emotional aspects of our being are all housed in our physical body, every bit of healing work that we do on the other three levels is reflected in our physical health and well-being. Our body is where we integrate and express all four levels of our existence. All the consciousness we gain on the other levels shows up in how alive we feel in our daily life. As the other levels are healed, our consciousness is freed to be more present in the moment. We naturally feel more in touch with our body and we are able to live in it more fully.

Of course, the physical body has its own specific healing process as well. As with the other levels, there are certain basic principles, common to everyone, yet each person's needs are unique as well.

In modern civilization, we are not generally encouraged to respect or be sensitive to our physical bodies. In fact, many of us are quite disconnected from our true physical needs. We can see clear evidence of this in the sedentary, non-physical lives of many modern urban dwellers. We see it in the concrete jungles and ugly towns, cities, and suburbs we humans seem prone to create everywhere we go. Millions of people are living and working every day in buildings that completely cut them off from anything natural. Many of these buildings don't even have natural light or air. And worst of all, we are polluting our air and water and are dumping toxic chemicals that saturate the soil in which we grow our food.

Just as our own physical bodies are physical manifestations and vehicles for our individual consciousness, so the earth is the physical manifestation and home for our collective consciousness. Thus, our awareness of, and relationship to the physical plane is reflected to us both in how we treat our own bodies and how we treat our Earth body.

One reason we are experiencing disconnectedness from our physical being has to do with the increasing emphasis on the intellect over the past few hundred years, and most particularly in the 20th century. Our eagerness to explore the mental level, and the resulting development of the technological age, has tended to cut us off from awareness of our natural physical selves.

Another contribution to the problem of disconnecting from the physical has been the attitude toward the body fostered by the traditional, transcendent spiritual approach, embraced by most world religions. The body is seen as the enemy of spirit, the seat of human needs, emotions, attachments, and passions. And it is the goal of these religions to subdue and rise above these human aspects. Therefore, the body is seen as lowly—inferior to mind and spirit, or even downright evil. Thus, our bodies are ignored or denigrated.

We are all born with a natural awareness of our bodies' needs and feelings, but we have learned to literally tune out the body. We may ignore it completely except when it's in extreme distress, so the body quickly learns that it has to get sick or have an accident in order to get attention. And even then, the attention we give may be in the form of trying to mask or get rid of the symptoms as quickly as possible so that we can resume our unconscious life patterns again. We learn to avoid looking deeper to discover the root of the problem—what the body is really trying to communicate to us.

Still, there are many of us who think we're paying a lot of positive attention to our physical health because we are interested in nutrition, exercise, and perhaps stress reduction. All too often, however, we are pushing our bodies to do the things we have mentally decided should be good for us—following a rigid diet or driving ourselves to perform a strenuous exercise program—rather than listening to the real messages our bodies are trying to give us. Even conscious relaxation programs, designed to reduce stress in our lives, can be used to block out the body's messages rather than becoming more conscious of them.

One of the major things making it possible to shut out our bodies' signals so effectively is the use of drugs. Most of us are becoming aware of the epidemic of drug, alcohol, tobacco, food, and other addictions we are currently suffering as people frantically try to cope with their emotional and spiritual pain by shutting it out. Fortunately, as we realize the futility and destructiveness of this method of dealing with our problems, more and more people are reaching out and finding healing. In fact, this may be the way a majority are getting involved with transformational processes—through twelve-step programs such as Alcoholics Anonymous and other treatment modalities.

Still, we remain a drug-oriented society, prone to cutting off our bodies' communications to us by popping a pill or ingesting a substance. One of the most insidious addictions, because it is largely unrecognized as a real problem, is the use of coffee. It is available everywhere. Huge numbers of people use it, and it constantly revs up the nervous system so that we can't possibly feel or follow our natural energy.

Because we've abdicated responsibility for our own bodies' well-being, we have become overly dependent on outside authorities when it comes to physical health. Of course, we must seek help from doctors and other professional health practitioners when we are in need of expert assistance, but we need to balance our reliance on others with self-awareness and self-trust as well. We need to see our helping professionals not as ultimate authorities but as "resource people" assisting us on our healing path.

A friend of mine went to a doctor who had been highly recommended concerning a growth on her foot. The doctor advised surgery. My friend had the operation, which proved unsuccessful. She was in considerable pain for some time. Another doctor she consulted said he would not have advised the surgery. My friend realized that she had not even paused to consider her own feelings or decide whether to get a second opinion before following the first doctor's advice. I'm not implying that a second opinion is always indicated; rather, I'm suggesting that it is just as important to check into our own sense of things as it is to check what the experts say.

The overall process of physical healing takes place in our lives as we learn to feel, listen to, and trust our bodies again. Our bodies often know what they need. They communicate to us clearly and specifically, if we are willing to listen to them. We must cultivate the art of understanding and interpreting their signals accurately.

Our bodies communicate their physical needs—what and when they desire to eat, how and when they desire rest or movement or physical contact from other people. Once we move through artificial, addictive cravings that we may have developed—using alcohol, drugs, caffeine, sugar, over-eating, overexercising, etc.—and get down to the body's true desires and responses, we have a very reliable guide for our physical needs. When we learn to listen to our bodies and heed their messages, we are well on the way to healing.

Keep in mind that your body is also an important bellwether of your spiritual, mental, and emotional needs. If you have ignored a need on another level — say, you have not paid attention to a yearning you have been feeling for spiritual nurturing — your body will eventually manifest that need in a physical form, say, in the form of constant headaches or perhaps an upper respiratory infection. This seems especially true of the feeling level, perhaps because this is the most blocked or neglected area for most of us; if we have not taken care of our emotional needs and feelings, they eventually try to get through to us through physical discomfort and disease. My personal belief is that most, if not all, of our physical ailments are related to spiritual, mental, and emotional causes.

Generally, an illness or accident is an indication that we may need to look a little deeper at our own needs and feelings, or pay more attention to following our inner guidance. It may be the symptom of an inner conflict that we need to deal with more directly. For example, my friend and business manager, Kathy Altman, is a wonderfully nurturing and responsible person. She is great at taking care of my needs and everyone else's but not so good at allowing herself to receive help from others. Once when we were organizing a large retreat in Hawaii she injured her ankle and was unable to handle all the logistics herself. She was forced to ask for help and support from others. This was difficult but, of course, healing for her. And everyone else was delighted to have the opportunity to care for her a bit.

The fact that physical ailments may be linked to emotional or other causes *does not mean that because we have an ailment we have failed to become a conscious person!* Too often, people who embrace the idea that physical diseases have roots in spiritual, mental, and emotional causes use this idea to beat themselves up. They feel that if only they had properly done their inner work, they could have prevented the problem.

Unfortunately, all too many teachers and healers unintentionally support these feelings of shame or guilt by implying that thinking the right thoughts, saying the right affirmations, eating the right diet, or whatever, ought to keep you perfectly healthy. Needless to say, it's not so simple. We can eat a pure diet, meditate every day, exercise regularly, express our feelings often, use affirmations and visualization, and still get sick! The consciousness process is complex and often mysterious. We can't always know exactly why something is happening. Remember that our soul uses every avenue available to educate and enlighten us.

A physical ailment is not necessarily a negative occurrence. In fact, it is always an opportunity for learning, growth, and healing on all levels—not only for the person with the ailment, but also for the loved ones who are affected by it. This is true for minor or major illnesses or accidents, although of course the more serious the problem, the greater the intensity of the learning. As difficult as it can be to accept, any ailment can be viewed as a gift, an opportunity to look at ourselves and our lives and learn something. It presents a possibility for real change and movement.

The most constructive and effective way to deal with an ailment is to acknowledge that you have it, that you are not "guilty" for having it, but that you wish to use the experience to deepen and expand your consciousness.

Naturally, it doesn't usually feel like an opportunity for change and growth at the time. Most likely, it feels painful, frightening, confusing, discouraging. Part of the healing process is to allow ourselves to experience those feelings. It can be helpful to put a kind of framework around the experience, one that goes something like this: "Even though this feels terrible and I don't understand it, I know that there is a gift of learning and healing for me here, and I'm open to receiving that and understanding it at the appropriate time."

This empowers our inner guidance to show us what we need to learn from the experience.

For example, I was recently ill with a virulent flu—the virus from Hell! For months I'd been under a lot of pressure, which included writing this book. When I got the flu, I was still under as much pressure as ever, but I felt too sick to do anything but lie in bed. It was stressful to feel myself falling behind in my responsibilities. I had no energy to cope with anything—a strange feeling, for I am generally healthy and energetic.

As the symptoms lingered for almost two weeks, I found myself falling into a deep depression, in which some very dark feelings of hopelessness and meaningless came to the surface. Finally, with the help of a therapist friend, I was able to get in touch with the underlying emotions. I had been driving myself so hard for two or three months, trying to do so much (which tends to be my pattern), that my inner child had become hopeless and discouraged, convinced that she would never again have any rest, nurturing, or fun! Once I expressed these feelings, I felt much lighter emotionally, and the next day I was finally physically well.

Since then I have been able to balance my hard work with more rest and pleasure. This is an issue I have been working on for many years, and the illness seems to have taken me to a new level of healing. In addition, I gained tremendous understanding and empathy for those who suffer from depression. I had rarely experienced this feeling of not being able to cope with life, and now I know how frightening and debilitating it can be. This can only help me be a more compassionate and skilled facilitator for others suffering from similar symptoms.

The illness I had was clearly a combination of physical (there was a terrible virus going around) and emotional factors (I was stressed out and needed a break.) I don't know which came first, the virus or the overwork, but clearly they worked together. The result is that I received a gift. And now

I feel great! So this was not an experience I could or should have avoided. It was a perfect step on my journey.

Obviously, with a life-threatening illness or accident, the stakes are higher, the feelings much more intense. The opportunities for growth are also that much more powerful. Many people discover that a critical illness causes them to confront major issues and through this confrontation gain life-changing awareness.

Again, we need to be careful about judging ourselves or others for having a serious illness or for any of the results that follow. We need to understand that death can be a legitimate and positive choice, not a failure to heal. Who are we to judge the journey of our own or another's soul? A life-threatening illness may cause one person to choose life and make any necessary changes to heal themselves. Another person may consciously or unconsciously choose death. Perhaps they have accomplished what they needed in this life, or they feel that they'll be able to accomplish the next step more effectively on a different plane of existence, or in another lifetime.

A friend of mine recently related the story of his mother's death to me. He told of sitting with her through the last few weeks of her life, beginning when she was in severe denial about her terminal illness all the way through to her very peaceful and conscious death. Being in her mid-80s, she felt that she had accomplished everything she had ever dreamed of doing and she was quite content with her life. She had a very large tumor growing in her pancreas and one day when her doctor touched it and asked her if she was feeling any pain, she replied with a smile, "Oh, no. I am grateful for it. It is letting me leave this life and go on."

If you are suffering from a critical illness, one of the most important things you can do is try to get in touch with, and acknowledge, that part of you that wants to die and is choosing death. Find out why it is making this choice. Allow the feeling its full expression. You may also need to feel and acknowledge that part of you that wants to live. Find out why it is making that choice. Allow yourself to consciously feel the conflict between the two; then, sit with the unresolved conflict for as long as you need to until it begins to resolve itself in some way. You may need support and facilitation from a therapist or counselor experienced in this field to do this.

It may be shocking to think that you have a part of you that *wants* to die. You may not be consciously in touch with this part at all. Few of us are. However, in my experience, anyone dealing with a life-threatening illness has a part of their psyche choosing death, consciously or unconsciously. Often, it has its roots in the vulnerable child within, who is somehow not getting his or her needs met. Sometimes this has to do with a very heavy inner critic or inner tyrant who is generating a feeling of self-hate.

In some cases the body itself can be feeling unappreciated and unsupported, perhaps because the person has a transcendent spiritual philosophy and considers the body unimportant, unreal, or even corrupt. Or there may be a spiritual aspect that simply feels ready to move on, as with my friend's mother in the anecdote above. By getting in touch with the parts that want to die and the parts that don't, it's possible to make the choice a more conscious one.

One of the best techniques for doing this work is the Voice Dialogue process, described in the chapter, "Discovering Your Many Selves." You might also try journal writing or writing with your non-dominant hand. (Please see the books by Deena Metzger and Lucia Capacchione, which I list in the Recommended Resources section in the back of this book.) Of course, use these techniques in conjunction with whatever medical and/or healing care you need.

◆ ◆ ◆

How do we go about healing the physical level of our being? The first step, especially if we have an acute or serious ailment, is to get the most immediate and effective treatment we can find. (See discussion below.) The second step is to learn more about ongoing ways to maintain and strengthen our physical health. This might include treatment and support from the appropriate medical and/or alternative practitioners. The third step, which can be done simultaneously with the first and second, is to look into the emotional, mental and spiritual factors that may contribute to the physical problem, then get whatever help you might need to heal those areas.

Choosing a treatment method for a physical problem can be confusing. In this day and age, we have many choices available—including: Western medicine and surgery, classic Chinese medicine, Ayurvedic medicine, homeopathy, herbology, naturopathy, acupuncture, chiropractic, massage and bodywork, exercise therapies, as well as diet and nutrition.

My personal feeling is that all these modalities and others I may have failed to mention, do have value and are appropriate in particular situations. I have benefited from nearly all of them at certain times in my life. Many of them, such as hatha yoga, exercise, massage, chiropractic care, acupuncture, and good nutrition, are part of my regular health-maintenance regime.

Increasingly, we are finding that there are medical doctors and clinics throughout the country who work with both mainstream medicine and alternative methods. Such people can be invaluable resources when faced with a serious illness. They can be tremendously helpful in providing you with the information you will want when making choices that have to do with your treatment.

It's important to find out what works for you, whether it's for maintaining good health, treating problems when they arise, or for restoring strength and health following radical treatment such as surgery. In my experience, the more acute the problem, the more likely it is that Western medicine will be called for, since it generally employs the strongest and fastest methods for dealing with immediate symptoms or the disturbance of a normal physical function. For subtler problems, some of the so-called alternative methods may actually be more effective. For example, Western medicine may not be able to help when it comes to many back problems but by working with a chiropractor, massage therapist and/or body worker, we can slowly heal and retrain the physical body so that the problem doesn't recur. In many cases, the skill, wisdom, and sensitivity of the practitioner may be a more important factor than the method they use.

Explore, discover, and learn as much as you can about the alternatives available to you, then trust your inner guidance about what's best for you. Seek the advice of appropriate professionals. Really listen to what they have to say. Take in feedback from friends and loved ones. Then listen deeply to your own sense of truth and make your own decisions about the best course of action.

Having done what you need to do to make sure your body is getting the care it needs, turn your attention to the other levels of your being. Find out what you need emotionally, mentally, and spiritually. Then take steps to care for those needs.

Remember that our bodies are wonderful communicators. They let us know what they need. Cultivate the art and practice of feeling, sensing, and listening to what your body is saying. As we learn to respond to our bodies' needs, we gradually become attuned to our own natural rhythms and those of the Earth.

Mother Earth is our greatest teacher. If we pay attention we can learn from her everything we need to know about living on the physical plane. Every day, in every way, she demonstrates to us her natural rhythms and cycles, all the natural laws of life.

Most of the indigenous cultures of the world had a deep understanding and reverence for humanity's connection with the earth. Their belief systems were built around the essential connections between our "Mother Earth" and our physical, emotional, mental, and spiritual wellbeing both collectively and individually. The current resurgence of interest in the wisdom of indigenous peoples reflects a recognition that we have a great deal to learn from them about creating healthy relationships with ourselves, each other, and the Earth.

The pressures of modern life tend to move us further and further from the natural cycles and rhythms of the Earth. We get up when the alarm clock rings; we go to bed after the eleven o'clock news. Life is structured according to what we *think* needs to be done, not according to our sensitivity to a natural rhythm. Yet, separated though we may be, we are still part of the Earth. We need to acknowledge that, to respect the Earth's rhythms and live in accordance with them.

We are not machines that can produce the same output each and every day, endlessly. Our mental and emotional states are different on sunny summer days than they are on cloudy winter days. And there are a myriad of other subtle changes throughout the day that affect us. If we can acknowledge and accept these differences each day, we can move more within the flow of life.

In order to get more in touch with our Earth connections, it is essential to be outside a little every day, even if it is just for a few moments. It is only by having that direct contact with the natural world that we can become conscious of the subtle changes occurring throughout the year. If you live in the city, it's a little more difficult to stay in touch with nature, but almost anyone can walk outside, observe the sky and feel the sun and the air.

Daily physical movement is an important part of maintaining a healthy, happy body and soul. As we move our bodies, the life-force can flow freely through, healing and replenishing our physical form and bringing us pleasure and joy.

I am convinced that life in a physical body is meant to be an ecstatic experience. Through commitment to our healing and to our transformational process we can open to more and more of life's many gifts.

EXERCISE
Moving Meditation

Find a time when you can have some privacy in your home. (That may be a challenging enough exercise right there, for most people!) Move the furniture aside, if necessary, to make some space for yourself in a room where you can have a tape player. Then try this moving meditation.

Pretend that your body is a musical instrument tuning up in preparation for playing in an orchestra. Select some of your favorite music and start to move to it gently.

You may want to pay attention to your body's natural order, starting with moving your head for a minute or two, following the rhythm of the music.

Next, switch to your shoulders and move them any way you choose, staying with them for a few minutes.

Follow each part of your body for a few minutes until you feel that part has been given enough time to warm up and express itself—your arms, hands, chest, hips, thighs, knees and feet.

When you reach your feet, you might want to work back up in the reverse order—knees, thighs, hips, etc.—for further warm-up. When you feel you have "tuned up your instrument," begin to let your whole body move spontaneously to the music. Imagine that the music is actually moving throughout you, that your body is being "played" like an instrument by the sound.

Try this exercise for at least twenty minutes per day for one week and see how different you feel. Note which parts of your body are expressive. Which ones feel tight? Give each part time for expression and you will notice them begin to change.*

Communicating with Your Body

If you have an ache or pain in, let's say, your lower back, sit quietly and actually imagine that this part of your body is able to talk to you. Ask it what it wants or needs. Ask it what it would like you to know. Sit and listen for answers that will come to you as an idea, an imagined voice, or perhaps in a dream or daydream. You might also try journal writing, with your non-dominant hand representing the voice of your body, or any part of your body.

This exercise is one of the best ways I know to begin developing good communications with your body. As you learn more and more about feeling, sensing, and listening to what it is telling you, you will begin to discover not only what your body needs but how to get to the real source of your discomfort or illness, which is the first step toward lasting health and balance.

If you wish to learn more about these skills, you will find *Passion to Heal*, by Echo Bodine, very helpful. It is listed in the Recommended Resources chapter at the end of this book.

---

* Adapted from the work of Gabrielle Roth, author of *Maps to Ecstasy: Teachings of an Urban Shaman*. She has also produced some excellent music tapes which are great for doing this exercise. See the Recommended Resources section.

INTEGRATION

There is a simple universal principle: Everything in the universe wants to be accepted. All aspects of creation want to be loved and appreciated and included.

A key word on the path of transformation is "integration." Simply stated, this means "joining together into one functional whole." Within our present context, it means becoming more fully realized beings, developing, expressing, and embodying all aspects of god/universe/life as fully as possible in our daily lives. Living on earth successfully means embracing and integrating our animal (physical), human (emotional and mental), and divine (spiritual) selves.

The physical world is a plane of duality. It contains infinite polarities, meaning that for every truth there seems to be an equal and opposite truth. For minds like ours, influenced by the highly technological, linear thought systems of the late 20th century, the existence of dualities — wherein every truth has its polar opposite — seems paradoxical and difficult to comprehend. To understand the whole and not be confused by the dualistic world we have made, we need to draw from our more intuitive, right-brained, holistic selves which aren't troubled by the fact that truth can seem paradoxical and are quite comfortable with exploring polarities.

For every essential energy within us, there is potentially an equal, opposite energy to balance it—for example, doing and being, giving and receiving, power and vulnerability. The more we can develop and embrace these opposites of life within ourselves, the more conscious, integrated, and balanced we become. Life is always guiding us in the direction that will help us develop the qualities that we most need.

In order to fully express one energy, it is necessary to integrate its opposite. It can even be said that the way to one quality is through its opposite. For example, you truly have strength only to the degree that you've accepted and embraced its opposite—your weakness or vulnerability. Just as being a good teacher requires us to be willing to learn, so to be truly wise we must learn to accept our own foolishness.

Most of us are very good at accepting and expressing one side of any given polarity, not so good at accepting and expressing the other side. One person might be comfortable in a leadership role but be unable to accept a subordinate position; another person might be comfortable as a follower but not as a leader. Or, one might stay in the safe middle ground, afraid to explore either extreme—i.e., unable to lead or follow. If we're identified with one polarity, life frequently pushes us toward its opposite. If we're only comfortable in the middle, it may guide us first in one direction and then the other.

If we wish to integrate our inner polarities we can't reject any parts of ourselves, not even the ones we're not yet comfortable with. Integration means expanding to include them. We judge some of our feelings, thoughts, and energies as negative, and we classify other aspects of ourselves and life in general as positive. We attempt to get rid of the negative things and experience only the positive ones. But the things we call negative are just the things we're afraid of or don't really understand. We don't want to experience them and so we try to get rid of them. But they can never go away because they are part of us and part of life.

Blocking what we have defined as "negative" aspects of ourselves requires a huge amount of energy and this means that we are robbing ourselves of our potential power. By spending more and more of our energy trying to keep the door shut on our "negative" selves, trying not to experience aspects that we think are negative and frightening, we drain our life force. We can actually die from using our energy to close off our energy!

Life is trying to teach us how to open the door and begin to look at those parts of ourselves that we've been frightened of, that we've hated, that we think are bad and ugly and awful and scary. Life is helping us to discover the hidden aspects of ourselves that we need, that we want, that we can't really live without.

There is a simple universal principle: Everything in the universe wants to be accepted. All aspects of creation want to be loved and appreciated and included. So, any quality or energy you are not allowing yourself to experience or express will keep coming up inside you, or around you, until you recognize it as a part of you, until you accept it and integrate it into your personality and your life.

If, for instance, you were taught that it is wrong and bad to express anger, and you never allowed yourself to do that, you would have a lot of anger building up inside you. Eventually, it would come out in an explosion, or it would cause you to feel depressed, or it might contribute to the development of a physical illness. Also, you would find that you were attracting angry people into your life, or your mate or one of your children might be very angry. Once you learned to express your anger in appropriate and constructive ways, however, it can empower and enr;ich your life. You would likely find the people in your life less angry as well.

Whatever we don't like, whatever we reject, whatever we try to get away from or get rid of, will haunt us. It will bug us. It will follow us around and fly right in our face. It will pursue us in our dreams. It will cause problems in our life through our relationships, our health, our finances, until we are willing and able to confront it, recognize it, and embrace it as a part of ourself. Once we do that, it's no longer a problem. It's no longer a big deal. It no longer runs our life. We begin to have an increasingly large range of choices and possibilities.

How, exactly, do we go about the integration process I describe here? That's what the next few chapters are about.

DISCOVERING
OUR MANY SELVES

The fact is that within each personality are many different sub-personalities, or selves. To better understand our own inner conflicts and inconsistencies we need to become aware of these.

As modern, civilized adults, we expect ourselves to feel and behave in a rational, consistent manner most of the time. But the fact is that our feelings and behavior are often quite inconsistent from one hour or day to the next. For example, we may feel quite clear and confident at one point in time, and at another moment feel completely the opposite—insecure, confused, uncertain. Furthermore, we often experience inner conflict, whether consciously or unconsciously. Maybe one part of us wants to make a radical change in our life, like leaving a job or a relationship, while another part wants to keep the status quo. Or there may be a part that wants to work hard and succeed, while a conflicting part wants to relax and take it easy.

The fact is that within each personality are many different sub-personalities, or selves. To better understand our own inner conflicts and inconsistencies we need to become aware of these. The process of consciousness growth involves getting to know our many inner selves and bringing them into balance and integration in our personalities.

The universe consists of an infinite number of essential qualities, energies, and archetypes. As spiritual beings, each of us is a microcosm of the macrocosm—containing bits of all that exists in the universe. When we are born into physical bodies, we have the potential for developing and expressing all of these energies in our human personality.

The formation of personality can be imagined as being somewhat like the different skins of an onion. At the core is our essential spiritual being, with additional layers growing around that core as we experience the world and begin to develop ways of functioning within it. The first layer of personality to develop around that essential core is the infant. The infant continues to be very closely connected to the spiritual self, so it is intensely aware and sensitive, with a tremendously powerful and magnetic presence.

On the physical level, the tiny infant is completely helpless, vulnerable, and dependent. In order to survive, it must attract the love and care of the mother, family, and/or other people around it. So it begins to experiment with expressing itself in different ways, soon discovering which expressions produce the best results. It may discover that smiling and cooing bring love and warmth, and crying when it's uncomfortable also brings the needed attention. Or it may find that when it cries it gets ignored or even punished.

As the child grows, it continues to experiment with a variety of energies and behaviors. It watches parents and others in the environment, and imitates them. The behaviors that bring approval and reward, or that allow it to escape punishment or the pain of abandonment, are incorporated into the personality, becoming another layer of the onion. Energies and expressions that produce disapproval, or which go unrewarded by the outside world, or that bring unwelcome attention such as criticism, ridicule or punishment, are eventually scrapped or repressed and do not become an obvious part of the outward personality. Though they may be eliminated from the everyday personality, these expressions don't necessarily go away. Instead, they may very well go underground and remain undeveloped, or they can pop out at unguarded moments.

This process of developing and expressing certain aspects of ourselves while repressing or disowning others continues throughout our childhood, adolescence, and adulthood. The energies that we feel most comfortable expressing become our primary selves—the dominant parts of the personality. We become closely identified with our primary selves, and think that that's who we are. In fact, until we become conscious of this process of personality development, our primary selves really run our lives.

For example, in my family, intellectual pursuits were highly valued and rewarded with positive attention, so I developed primary selves that are rational and articulate. My mother was a strong role model, being a powerful, adventurous, and successful career woman. So I developed primary selves that were similar to hers—strong, competent, hardworking, and willing to take risks. Since my parents were divorced when I was three, and my mother needed to work, I developed a sense of responsibility and independence very early. As a sensitive child, I could feel my parents' (and others') emotional pain, and I tried to give them support. So even as a young girl, the caretaking mother energy in me became a strong primary self.

How we describe ourselves, or how someone who knows us well describes us, is usually a pretty good description of our primary selves. If I were asked to describe myself as a young adult, I would probably have said that I was intelligent, responsible, serious, outgoing, and caring.

Our primary selves are very strong, real energies. They are like people that live inside us and make almost all our decisions. Their underlying purpose is to protect and defend the vulnerable child energy that still lives deep within us—the first layer of the onion. Usually we are quite unaware that we have a vulnerable child inside of us, and that much of our behavior is rooted in the unconscious attempt to meet this child's needs and protect it from harm. We are also largely unaware of our primary selves as distinct energies. We are so totally identified with them we think that's who we really are.

Our primary selves may occupy ninety percent (or even more) of our personality and our time; even so, these selves are only a part of who we actually are. The primary selves developed as the best way we could find to survive and succeed in our family and cultural environment. They are the energies that were the most successful at getting our early needs met.

We have many other energies, often very different or seemingly the opposite of our primary selves, that were neglected or repressed in the past because they failed to get us the attention and approval we wanted, or because they actually gained us disapproval or punishment from our family, teachers, or community. Since these energies are nevertheless a natural part of us, they don't go away just because we don't express them. They remain inside us, totally dormant, or perhaps pushing their way out at moments when our primary selves are off guard. These repressed or undeveloped energies are our disowned selves.

In my case, since my primary selves are serious, responsible, and hardworking, some of my disowned energies would be carefree, lighthearted, and playful. Since I'm such a "doer," a less developed energy in me is the ability to relax and just "be."

Our disowned selves are just as important to us as our primary selves. They represent our potential for expanding, developing, and expressing ourselves in new ways. They are not negative, though they may seem that way to us at first. They may have become distorted through being repressed for so long. So when we become aware of a disowned self within us, it may seem very negative or frightening at first. But as we get more in touch with it, allow it to express itself, and come to understand it, we see that at its root, it is a positive, natural quality that is necessary to our well-being and wholeness.

For example, if you are very identified with a primary self which is kind, considerate, and loving, you might very well discover that one of your disowned selves is just the opposite—selfish and seemingly uncaring of others. These qualities no doubt sound very negative to you, and you wonder, "Why would I want to develop and embrace that part of myself? I don't want to be selfish and thoughtless of others. In fact, I'd like to get rid of that part of me completely."

However, you can't get rid of any part of you. You can deny it and repress it, in which case it will eventually cause problems in your life. Or you can acknowledge and accept it as a natural, human part of you, in which case it is no longer such a big deal. And consider this: if your primary self is caring, considerate, and giving to others ninety percent of the time, you are probably giving far too much. This will eventually drain you so there is nothing left to give.

Giving too much is not really good for you or anyone else, because you are out of balance. Getting in touch with and owning the opposite quality of selfishness—i.e., being aware of your *own* needs and taking care of them—would provide you with the balance that you need. By learning to take care of yourself better, you will actually have more to give to others.

Embracing your disowned selves does not mean becoming totally identified with them or displacing your primary selves. It means finding an appropriate balance between the two so that your life works better and you feel more integrated, more whole.

Another word for our disowned selves is our "shadow." A shadow self is simply any part of us that we have not recognized and accepted. Since that self is a part of us, it can't go away just because it has been rejected. So it follows us through life like our shadow, until we notice and acknowledge it.

For many of us, the aspects of ourselves that we are most likely to disown are the instinctual energies—those associated with our sexuality and the aggressive drives. One reason for this is that most of us learn very early that these drives are feared and distrusted by civilized society and often condemned by traditional religion. Since these energies are powerful expressions of the life force itself, when we disown them we end up repressing a great deal of our natural vitality. The repression of these forces—a key source of chronic stress—can eventually lead to emotional depression and physical illness. Embracing these energies does not mean we turn them loose to run rampant in our lives. It means finding a balance where we can acknowledge, appreciate, and enjoy our instinctual selves while maintaining our awareness of consideration for others, the need for boundaries, appropriateness of our behavior, and so on.

Our culture places such a high value on strength and self-sufficiency that many of us disown or deny any feelings of need we may have. It's hard for us to admit that we need or want help or support from anyone. Any feelings of need or dependency seem very shameful. Yet, without the ability to accept and acknowledge our feelings of need and vulnerability, we can't reach out for help when appropriate, we can't receive love, we can't embrace our humanity. Instead, we develop primary selves that are super-competent, independent, and distrustful of others. This predicament has been most typical of men in the traditional male role, but in the past few decades it has increasingly become a woman's problem as well.

At the opposite pole, some people become closely identified with need and vulnerability. If these qualities become a person's primary self, they lose all sense of strength and independence. This personality structure develops because the person discovers early in life that expressing power is dangerous or incurs criticism. It's safer or more comfortable to be vulnerable, dependent, passive. Without access to their power to assert themselves and take care of themselves, these highly dependent people can become victimized by others. Traditionally, this has been more common for women but in these changing times many men find themselves with this problem, too.

How do we find balance and integration between our primary and our disowned selves? The first and most important step is to become aware of and identify our primary selves. The very act of noticing them as parts of us means that we have taken a step away from being so totally identified with them that we are literally swallowed up by them. While perhaps seeming subtle, this step is, in fact, extremely powerful. Remember that the major part of change comes from awareness.

As we become more aware of the primary selves we begin to develop an aware ego—a conscious part of our personality—which knows about all the various selves and helps to orchestrate balance and harmony. As our recognition of our primary selves increases, so also do the choices we have in our lives. For example, when I was able to see my hardworking, intellectual energies as primary selves, I also began to see that there were other possibilities. Life didn't have to be all hard work. The fact is that as long as I clung only to these qualities, acting as if they absolutely had to be followed at all times, other aspects of myself were neglected.

As we develop an aware ego which is able to observe the primary selves with more objectivity and detachment, we find ourselves becoming much more open to a wider and wider range of choices. As we separate from complete identification with our primary selves, our disowned energies begin to filter into the space that is created. They will do this gradually and naturally, so that we simply begin to feel more and more balanced. Once the aware ego has developed, our lives tend to be much more relaxed and open, and we become quite comfortable with those selves we previously denied or repressed.

This doesn't mean that we try to get rid of our primary selves. On the contrary, they are vital parts of us that we still need! They've helped us survive and get this far in life. We want to keep them with us. The increased consciousness provided by our aware ego simply gives us a greater range of conscious choices about our lives. Instead of having my hardworking responsible self running ninety-five percent of my life, and making almost all my decisions for me, I prefer to have it as a trusted advisor. Then I may gradually begin choosing to work hard and be responsible a little less, and allow my disowned energies of relaxation, carefreeness, and play come into my life, enriching it.

In this process it is quite important to appreciate and acknowledge our primary selves for all that they have done to take care of us, and let them know we still want them. This may sound strange, but the sub-personalities are like real people who have the need to be loved, understood, appreciated, and included. They have a job to do and they don't want to be disregarded. If they feel that we are trying to get rid of them or undermine them, they will fight back hard, and often in very devious ways, sabotaging our efforts to grow and change. Every part of us is important and needs to know it will have its rightful place in our psyche and our lives.*

---

* Readers may wonder how the concept of many selves relates to multiple personality disorder. To simplify, we all have many different selves or sub-personalities within us. However, if a person suffers severe abuse or trauma in early life, these energies may fragment into many different parts, with very little holding them together and little or no awareness of one another. Thus, rather than having the various selves working together as a more or less integrated whole, as they do in relatively healthy personalities, the person with multiple personality disorder shifts from one self to an-

Underneath the complex structure of our personality, with all its primary and disowned sub-personalities, there lies the energy of the original vulnerable child we once were. Although we may have lost conscious touch with the child, it never grows up or goes away. It remains a deep part of us throughout our lives. Basically, our entire personality has developed in order to take care of the child, try to get its needs met, and protect it from harm. Paradoxically, the child usually gets buried beneath the multiple layers of our personality, forgotten at a conscious level. Unconsciously, however, most of the other selves are constantly attempting to take care of the child in various (often conflicting) ways.

As we gain awareness, we usually discover that many of the ways we've been trying to meet our inner child's needs are outdated, limited, or even self-destructive. For example, if we grew up in a dysfunctional family situation we may have developed a defensive posture to protect the child in us from getting hurt. We don't let anyone close to us emotionally. Later, we may become aware that this behavior is preventing us—and particularly our inner child—from getting the nurturing and love it wants or needs. As adults with aware egos, we can choose to change this pattern and allow certain people close to our inner child once again.

At this point, we have begun to take conscious charge of the process. But to do this we need to get acquainted with our inner child, find out how it feels and what it needs, and learn to consciously care for it in an effective way. In a sense we need to become aware, caring parents to our own child self.

Healing our relationship with our inner child is one of the most important and profound steps on our consciousness journey. Because the child is the deepest part of our

---

other, as if that was his or her only self. Fortunately, many who suffer from multiple personality disorder are finding healing through therapy.

personality, it is the key to our emotional well-being. Until we have conscious access to our sensitive, vulnerable child self, and are able to express its needs and feelings, we can't create and sustain true intimacy in our relationships. In addition to feeling deeply, the child is the part of us that knows how to play, have fun, and enjoy life. Without our playful child energy, life becomes too serious and drab.

Because the child is the first layer of personality, it is closely linked to our spiritual essence. Discovering and embracing our inner child opens the doorway to our soul. So our relationship with our inner child is the source of our creativity, natural wisdom, and our spiritual well-being.

◆ ◆ ◆

Much of my understanding about the many selves within us, and the importance of developing the aware ego, has come from studying and working with Drs. Hal and Sidra Stone. Their understanding of the psychology of selves is quite profound, and the method they have created for getting to know and understand our many sub-personalities—Voice Dialogue—is one of the most powerful tools for consciousness that I have ever experienced. Their work relates to and draws from many other disciplines—Jungian analysis, Gestalt therapy, Psychosynthesis, to name just a few. But it takes a few steps beyond anything else. I have found it extraordinarily helpful, both in my own personal healing process and in my work with others.

Hal and Sidra are wise and wonderful teachers who lead workshops and trainings all over the world. They are the authors of several excellent books and numerous tapes. (In the Recommended Resources section of this book, you'll find more information about their written and recorded material, as well as their workshops.)

Voice Dialogue is one very effective way of discovering and healing your inner child, and there are many other ways as well. These days, there are numerous support groups and therapists specializing in helping people do their inner child work. Al-Anon has special groups for Adult Children of Alcoholics or other dysfunctional family situations, with special focus on learning to love and care for your inner child. The books, seminars and television programs of John Bradshaw have helped millions of people understand the importance of doing their inner child work. There is an excellent book, *Recovery of Your Inner Child*, by Lucia Cappachione, Ph.D., which shows you how to get in touch with and heal your inner child through writing with your non-dominant hand. A dear friend of mine, Tanha Luvaas, has written a wonderful book, *Notes from My Inner Child: I'm Always Here*, which I highly recommend. The book was actually written by Tanha's inner child and strongly evokes the inner child of the reader. Also, I have a tape called *Discovering Your Inner Child* with a meditation to help you make contact with your inner child. All these items are listed more fully in the Recommended Resources section of this book.

EXERCISE

Getting Acquainted with Your Primary Selves

To get a sense of your primary selves, make a list of six to twelve of your strongest, and most obvious, personality characteristics. If you have difficulty identifying what these might be, think of a close friend who knows you well and imagine how he or she might describe you. Then jot down a list of those descriptive words. Try not to be judgmental or to evaluate your qualities in either a positive or negative way. Be as objective as possible.

Once you have made this list, take a look at it and see if it seems to describe your primary ways of operating in the world. As you become more aware of these, you might also become aware that your innermost feelings are not necessarily represented by these selves. For example, your primary selves might include ones that are aggressive, outgoing, and funny, while deep inside you feel shy, sad, and very "guarded" or "private."

If you think of any qualities you have that are not included in your list, add these. How do these primary selves operate in your life? For instance, you might see that one of your primary selves is a "good mother" or "good father," and the way it operates in your life is that it is very aware and caring of the needs of others, but may not be much in touch with the needs of your own inner child.

Now go through your list and for every primary quality listed, see if you can think of an opposite quality. Make two columns on a piece of paper, listing your primary quality in the first column, the opposite of that quality in the second. If you think of more than one opposite quality for a single primary quality, write them both down. If you can't think of an opposite word, just leave it blank. Here's an example of one person's list:

Primary Qualities	Opposites
Introverted	Outgoing
Intellectual	Emotional; Physical
Shy	Bold
Kind	Selfish
Organized	Spontaneous
Humorous	Serious
Hardworking	Lazy; Relaxed
Creative	?

If you find you have many negative or judgmental words in your second column, see if you can think of a positive way of describing that same quality. For example, in the list above the person wrote two words opposite "hardworking;" the first was "lazy," which has negative connotations, the second was "relaxed," which has positive associations. If you can't think of a positive synonym for the second column, let it go for now.

Look at the second column of words and see if some of them might describe disowned or less-developed selves. Then, ask yourself how you might benefit by developing those opposite qualities.

You may find you already have sets of opposite words in your *primary self* column. This may mean that you have developed some opposite primary selves, who may be in conflict within you.

Most people find they are most balanced and most effective in their lives when they are able to draw from both sides of any pair of opposites. How could you learn to accept and find balance between both sides of you?

One simple technique that can help you begin to accept your inner contradictions and find balance, is to come up with an *oxymoron* to describe two polarities within you. An oxymoron is a name that describes one person or thing that incorporates what may seem to be contradictory qualities, such as: "the hermit-extrovert;" "the selfish saint;" and "the spontaneous organizer." Play around with this idea until you find the label that describes these contradictory qualities and it will help you to both understand your gifts and choose situations where those gifts are best applied.

For example, one person described himself as a "hermit-extrovert" because he was most effective when he could work alone but in a way that involved him with a large group of people. In his profession, he was a creative engineer who was part of a team developing new products. While the team came together to compare notes once a week, most of his actual work was done at his home office more than a hundred miles from the company's main offices.

As you become more aware of your inner contradictions and polarities, don't feel that you need to resolve them, fix them, or immediately find perfect balance and integration. Uncomfortable though it may be, the important thing is to become *conscious* of what's going on inside you without trying to *control* it. The important thing is to start becoming more aware of your different selves and see how they work in your life. More balance and integration will happen over time.

OUR RELATIONSHIPS
AS MIRRORS

If we learn to see our relationships as the wonderfully accurate mirrors they are, revealing to us where we need to go with our own inner process, we can see much about ourselves that we would otherwise have a great deal of difficulty learning.

One of the biggest differences between the path of the material world, the path of transcendence, and the path of transformation is in how we view our relationships.

On the material path we see relationships as an end in themselves. We form relationships of various kinds in order to satisfy our needs for love, companionship, security, stimulation, sexual fulfillment, financial stability, and so on. Our focus tends to be on the external form of the relationship and on what is being exchanged, be it friendship, work, affection, respect, money, or security. Because we view relationships primarily in the light of getting needs met, we tend to try to control them, to try to make them the way we want them. Consciously or unconsciously, we try to manipulate other people in order to get what we want from them. The control we assert limits how we experience our relationships.

On the path of transcendence, relationships are often viewed as impediments that keep us from evolving beyond the physical form. Because our relationships bring out all of our human feelings, needs, and emotional attachments, they are seen as distractions and thus detrimental to our spiritual journey. People who are seriously committed to the transcendent path try to stay as unattached as possible. Since sexuality is such a strong force physically and emotionally, involving our animal instincts and human feelings, it is often looked upon as the opposite of spirituality. Therefore, many devotees of the transcendent path either take a vow of celibacy and avoid sex altogether, or they try to transmute it into a "higher" energy, following sacred disciplines that keep the experience focused on its spiritual aspects.

On the path of transformation we embrace both our humanness and our spirituality. Instead of attempting to escape or ignore them, we honor our human needs for relationship; we learn to be more conscious of how to communicate those needs and how to take good care of ourselves and each other in the process. We also recognize that we are spiritual beings, not limited to our human form and emotions, but connected to the unlimited oneness of the universe. Rather than denying our sexuality, we embrace it as one of the most important expressions of our life force.

On the path of transformation there is a further vital step we must take, one that allows us to have a different perspective on relationships than we would if we followed a material or spiritual path. On the transformational path we need to recognize that all our relationships can be powerful mirrors, reflecting back to us what we need to learn. When we learn how to use these reflections, our relationships can become one of the most powerful avenues we have for becoming conscious.

Our primary relationship is really with ourselves. Each of us is involved in developing all aspects of our being and bringing them into relationship with one another—becoming whole. Our relationships with other people constantly reflect exactly where we are in that process. For example, for many years I yearned to find the right man to be my life partner. I created many relationships with men who were unavailable or inappropriate in certain ways. Eventually, I realized they were reflecting my own inner ambivalence about committed relationship, and the ways that I didn't truly love myself. It was only after I did much deep emotional healing work, learning to truly love and be committed to myself, that I met a wonderful man who is now my husband.

If we learn to see our relationships as the wonderfully accurate mirrors they are, revealing to us where we need to go with our own inner process, we can see much about ourselves that we would otherwise have a great deal of difficulty learning. Any and every relationship in our lives can be a reflection to us in this way—our friends, co-workers, neighbors, our children and other family members, as well as our primary partners. Even an encounter with a stranger can sometimes be an important learning experience.

It's very difficult to look inside ourselves and see what's going on in there—particularly to see what we're unaware of. That's why it's important to look at our relationships as mirrors of our inner processes. Used in this way, relationships become one of the most valuable sources of healing and teaching in our lives. To understand how this works, we need to remind ourselves that we each, through our individual consciousness, create and shape how we experience external reality. This is as true in our relationships as in every other area of our lives, i.e., the relationships we create and shape reflect back to us what we are holding within our consciousnesses. We draw to us and are drawn to people who match and reflect some aspect of ourselves.

Generally, we find that the easiest people to get along with are those who reflect aspects of ourselves that we feel comfortable with and accept—reflections of our primary selves, or complimentary energies that we appreciate.

These are usually people who we consciously seek out or are drawn to in everyday friendship. If you are primarily a physically active person who loves sports, you may feel most comfortable with people who are similarly athletic. You may also enjoy a relationship with a friend who is somewhat more intellectual and less physical than you because it stretches your mind in a way that you accept and enjoy—i.e., it stimulates a less developed aspect of you in a way is comfortable and non-confrontational. It reflects that part of yourself that acknowledges a need to develop your intellectual side.

The people in our lives who make us uncomfortable, who annoy us, who we feel judgmental or even combative toward, reflect parts of ourselves that we reject—usually aspects of our disowned selves, the shadow side of our personality. If you are a gentle, softspoken person, you may be very irritated by a person who seems loud and pushy. Or if you are a direct, outspoken person you may feel uncomfortable with those who hold back and seem overly timid. The fact is that in both cases you are mirroring each other's disowned energies. The quiet person is being shown their undeveloped assertive side, and the aggressive person is being shown their undeveloped reflective side.

Oftentimes we find ourselves attracted to our opposites —people who have developed opposite qualities from the ones we most identify with. In these relationships, we are unconsciously seeking to become whole, drawn to people who express those energies that are undeveloped in our own personalities. On some level, we recognize that they have the potential to help us become more balanced.

People who express our opposite aspects can be our most powerful teachers if we allow them to be. But first we must acknowledge that they express what we want and need to develop in ourselves. Early in a relationship, we often sense that the other person is bringing us exactly what we need. It is, in fact, their differentness that is so attractive to us. However, unless we are able to acknowledge that this person is offering us a reflection of something we need to see in ourselves, the differentness that drew us to them can actually become a source of conflict. After a while, we may begin to resent them for the ways they are different and begin trying to change them to be more like us!

Of course, it's important in any relationship to learn constructive ways to communicate honestly about our needs, our likes and dislikes, and so forth. However, along with letting the other person know our feelings, including ways we might wish they would change, we need to remind ourselves that we brought them into our lives to teach and inspire us to develop new aspects of ourselves. Our challenge, then, is to be open to discovering the parts of ourselves that they mirror for us, and to learn how we can express those parts of ourselves more in our own lives. For example, Joanne really loved the fact that her friend Tina was a free spirit who loved to "go with the flow." However, it began to annoy her that Tina was often late for appointments. She needed to communicate to Tina her desire not to be kept waiting. At the same time, she needed to keep in mind that Tina was in her life to help her get more in touch with her own spontaneity.

One very common relationship problem is the conflict between order and spontaneity. Some years ago, this dynamic was the central dramatic premise for the very popular play, movie, and television series, "The Odd Couple." Almost any two people who live together get into this polarization—one of them is neat and one of them is messy. Their arguments focus on trying to get the other person to change. But seen from a transformational point of view, the real conflict is between the very structured, organized, linear side of ourselves and our more spontaneous, intuitive, and creative aspects. One person is playing out one side, and the other person is playing out the other side.

You can have endless conflicts between you and this other person until you recognize that person is mirroring your own inner confict and is showing you what you want or need to develop in yourself. On the transformational path, you seek the balance between those two extremes by developing those "opposite" aspects in yourself so that you become more whole. Interestingly enough, when you find more balance in yourself the other person will often shift into a more balanced place as well, even though he or she knows nothing about the process! This is because we are energetically linked and strongly affected by one another.

It is very common in a primary relationship for one person to want greater commitment, depth, and intimacy while the other wants more freedom, more space. This outer conflict mirrors essential polarities within each of us. We all want closeness, intimacy, and commitment; at the same time, we fear loss of freedom and individuality. If you have this kind of conflict in a relationship, take a look at what it might represent about these polarities in yourself.

Another conflict that often comes up in close relationships is that one of the people takes a more rational approach to life and is emotionally detached or aloof; the other may be highly emotional.

So, for example, if a very rational man finds himself with a very emotional woman, the message being mirrored to him is that he can become more whole by developing his emotional side, by getting more in touch with his feelings. And the message being mirrored to the woman is that she can become more whole by cultivating a more impersonal, detached, and rational energy that will give her life greater balance. If the two people don't begin to integrate their opposite energies—instead of trying to change each other—they will eventually polarize even further, the man becoming even more rational and the woman even more emotional.

Interestingly, as this occurs the "symptoms" of their need to develop the opposite side of themselves become more exaggerated and uncomfortable. In utter frustration, they may withdraw completely from each other, and from others in their lives who reflect their opposite aspects. They can begin to heal their relationships and their lives when they see their conflicts as mirrors. Either person can begin to break the impasse by taking steps to recognize their primary selves and develop their opposite side.

Not long ago, I worked with a woman whose relationship with her husband clearly illustrated this point. He was trained as a computer engineer and spent most of his hours at work focused on very rational, linear, mental activities. She was a nursery school teacher, where she worked with the emotions of very young children all day. Nancy described the early years of her marriage to Ken as "blissful." She had never felt more complete or whole. Ken's cool, detached way of approaching problems gave her a sense of calmness and security that her life alone had lacked.

In time, however, she began to feel that he was literally sucking her energy out of her. He retreated into his computer whenever she got emotional. She became nearly hysterical every time he tried to "explain away" what she was feeling. The chasm between them grew until she could barely stand to be in the same room with him. She accused him of being totally unable to deal with anything emotional; he accused her of being totally irrational, lacking any ability to "work things out."

Nancy began to learn to see Ken's behavior as a mirror, reflecting back to her what she needed to develop in herself. Rather than seeing her husband as her enemy—which she acknowledged that she had begun to do—she began to view him as her teacher. In time, the tension between them eased and the very same qualities that they had begun to hate in each other became valuable guides, pointing the way not only to a more harmonious relationship but to a greater sense of balance within themselves.

It can be difficult for us to recognize or accept that people we have problems with are actually mirroring for us the disowned parts of ourselves. One simple way to tell if you are doing this is to check in with your own feelings; if you are feeling very judgmental toward that person, the chances are very good that they are mirroring your shadow side. Underneath, you may be jealous. Perhaps this person is expressing a kind of energy that you hold back or don't allow yourself to express.

I feel it's important to remember that mirroring in the way I'm describing is very different than making the other person a "role model." A role model is a person whom we admire and want to emulate. But in mirroring, our own self-discovery and self-development is the goal; we're not trying to be like another person. The goal is to become more ourselves. The fact is that the person mirroring our own needs may be even more out of balance than we are. They certainly don't have to be people who we look up to, as we might do with a role model. We don't have to become like they are, or go to an extreme to discover our center. However, we may need to allow ourselves to develop a little more of that energy that we are seeing reflected back to us.

For example, if you are a quiet, reserved, perhaps overly modest and self-effacing person, you might feel judgmental toward someone who always seems to seize the center of attention. They may be mirroring that part of you that would like to receive more attention but is afraid to. It's not necessary to emulate this person, who may very well be out of balance in the opposite direction from you. Instead, allow that person to be a catalyst for your growth process. Try to see the *essence* of the quality that this person reflects to you—i.e., the desire for love and attention—and begin to investigate how you can nurture and express that part of yourself *in your own way.*

We avoid the things that we're afraid of because we think there will be dire consequences if we confront them. But the truly dire consequences in our lives come from avoiding things that we need to learn about or discover. We must instead learn to be more open and accepting of the things we're afraid of, whether it's exploring our emotions, or learning to balance our checkbook! Acceptance is simply a willingness to look at, confront, and understand something instead of pushing it away.

Acceptance doesn't mean that we have to allow things into our lives that aren't good for us. Obviously, we wouldn't go out and commit a crime because we believed there was something to be gained by learning to confront fears we have about such behavior. We don't become whole unless we recognize the need to set boundaries and be able to discriminate between what's right and not right for us.

Being willing to learn from our relationships does not mean that we should stay in situations that are not good for us. If a relationship is physically or emotionally abusive, what we have to learn from it is how to set boundaries and protect ourselves. This could mean going into couples counseling to seek real and lasting resolutions. Or it could mean leaving the relationship if that is the only way we could effectively take care of ourselves.

People can criticize or abuse us only to the degree that we accept or allow it. First we must take steps externally to take care of ourselves. Then we must look inside to heal the way that we criticize or abuse ourselves; out of the knowledge we gain in this way we can learn to love and support ourselves instead.

A woman I know was raised by an emotionally and physically abusive father. She developed an internal "abusive father" energy which told her constantly how worthless and undeserving she was. She married a man who mirrored her pattern of internal self-abuse, constantly criticizing and belittling her and occasionally hitting her. She tolerated the situation for years because to her it all seemed normal; she believed she deserved the abuse. Once she began therapy, she was able to recognize that her husband was reflecting her beliefs about herself. She gradually developed an ability to stand up for herself and eventually she left the relationship. After going hrough a deep emotional healing process, she eventually remarried, this time to a man who was kind and supportive, reflecting the way she had learned to treat herself.

For many of us, our relationships have been such a painful struggle that it's difficult to believe we could get to a place in our lives when all relationships are primarily supportive and satisfying. Yet, if we are willing to do our deep emotional work, our relationships can mirror every step of progress that we make in our relationships with ourselves. As we become more integrated our relationships become an incredible reflection of our aliveness, self-love, and self-expression.

The art and science of using our relationships as reflections of our consciousness process is fascinating and complex. In this chapter I have merely touched upon some of the basic ideas. In fact, I am planning to write my next book on this topic. Meanwhile, I highly recommend the book, *Embracing Each Other: Relationship as Teacher, Healer and Guide*, by Drs. Hal and Sidra Stone, as well as their tapes, *The Dance of Selves in Relationship* and *Understanding Your Relationships*. I also found the book, *Getting the Love You Want*, by Dr. Harville Hendrix interesting and helpful. These books and tapes are listed in the Recommended Resources section.

EXERCISE

Using the Mirror of Relationship

Difficulties we are having in our relationships often mirror parts of ourselves that we need to heal. Such difficulties may involve a family member, a close friend, a co-worker, or even people with whom we have only a brief encounter—such as a clerk in a store.

If you are having difficulty with a present relationship, or if you frequently encounter certain kinds of difficult people—for example, a domineering person or people who don't respect your boundaries—take a moment to look closely at what they are reflecting.

Begin by relaxing and perhaps meditating for a moment. Then bring to mind a difficult relationship.

For the next few minutes, pretend that this person exists only in your imagination, or that they have appeared to you in a dream. In real life this person may trigger painful, angry, or judgmental feelings in you. But as you do this exercise be aware that you are in complete control since for now this person exists only in your mind.

As you hold this person in your mind, ask them to tell you exactly what they mirror in you. You might say to them, "I know you are in my life to help me become more conscious of something in myself. Because the lesson is not yet clear to me, please repeat it one more time in a way that is a little easier for me to grasp."

Then let the person take on all the traits of the best, most loving teacher you've ever had. Open up an inner dialogue with them, as if they were completely helpful, friendly, honest, cooperative and articulate. Here are some samples of what you might say, ask or discuss:

"When I look at your reflection of me, I feel _____." (Get in touch with feelings such as anger, fear, being out of control, confused, etc.)

"Which *self* in me is reflected by the mirror you offer?"

"Is the difficulty I'm having with these reflections linked to traumatic or abusive experiences from my past? If so, what are they?"

Remember that the lessons we have to learn from other people are all essentially positive. That is, they are pointing the way toward how we can love and accept outselves more, or learn to express more of who we are. So if you get critical or negative feedback from this process, your "inner critic" is probably getting in the act. Go back and ask to understand how this can work for you in a positive way.

As a final part of this exercise, remember that your best, most fulfilling relationships are also valuable mirrors, reflecting your greatest gifts. So bring to mind a relationship you have with a very dear and trusted friend and ask which of your gifts are reflected by them.

THE WORLD
AS OUR MIRROR

If we have the courage to look at the social and political forces in the world as reflections of the forces at work within each of us, we can more effectively take responsibility not only for our own personal healing, but for the healing of our planet.

On the path of transformation we are concerned with not only our own personal process of healing and integration, but with the healing process going on in our world. We recognize the interrelationship between our individual consciousness journey and the evolution of the consciousness of humanity.

Just as the imbalances in our individual consciousness are reflected in our personal relationships and in the daily events of our lives, so the imbalances in the collective consciousness are reflected in our communities, our nation, our relationships with other countries, and our relationships to the earth. Since we are each a participant in the mass consciousness, influencing it and being influenced by it, the world itself becomes a mirror that helps us see ourselves more clearly and understand ourselves more deeply. If we have the courage to look at the social and political forces in the world as reflections of the forces at work within each of us, we can more effectively take responsibility not only for our own personal healing, but for the healing of our planet.

Again, I want to remind you that taking responsibility for our part in the creation of our world does not mean taking or assigning blame. Obviously, no single one of us, as an individual, is to blame for the problems that exist in the world. Nor are we to blame for our own personal circumstances or difficulties. Rather, as spiritual beings, we have each chosen to play an important part in the fascinating, unfolding process of evolution that is taking place on this planet. We are doing this for our own learning and empowerment, and we each have special gifts that are needed in this world.

As we discussed in the last few chapters, we have many different aspects within us, and we are all in the process of bringing those energies into balance and integration in our bodies, our personalities, and our lives. As we have seen, our inner conflicts are frequently reflected in the conflicts we experience in our personal relationships. We literally project our unconscious inner conflicts into our external environment. When they are mirrored back to us in difficulties with other people, or difficulties accomplishing some of the things we want in our lives, we thereby create the possibility for becoming more aware of these inner conflicts and healing them. The people with whom we are in conflict are usually mirroring some parts of ourselves with which we are uncomfortable or unresolved.

For example, a client of mine, Ray, had a long history of negative encounters with authority figures, including the police and the legal system. Through our work together, he recognized that he had rejected and disowned the structured, authoritarian part of himself because of a negative, conflicted relationship he had with his father, who strongly identified with these energies. Ray continued to attract to himself people and situations that forced him to confront the aspects of himself that he had avoided or tried to get rid of—his authoritarian shadow side. It's interesting to note, of course, that Ray's father had also created, in his son, an excellent mirror for him to see his own reflection. Ray was literally a reflection of his father's shadow, those energies of the older man which wanted to rebel against all rules and structure! Once Ray was able to recognize the value in having a certain amount of "law and order" in life, and could embrace the structured, authoritarian aspects of himself, he began to feel more understanding toward his father and developed better communication and more closeness with him before the older man died.

Just as the dramas of our personal relationships have their roots in our individual psyches, so the social and political events in our world are rooted in the spiritual and psychological workings of the mass consciousness in which each of us is a participant. Community, national, and international conflict is a mass projection of individual internal conflicts, and of the internal conflicts within the societies involved. These inner conflicts are projected onto other people, other races, other cultures, other religions, and then externalized in the form of disputes, wars, revolutions, riots, and other efforts to weaken or annihilate whoever or whatever mirrors our disowned energies.

Just as we each have an individual shadow, groups have a collective shadow consisting of those qualities and energies they have collectively denied or repressed. We can see that collective shadow in operation whenever a group or nation projects its disowned energies onto another race, ethnic group, or country, transforming it into a feared and dreaded enemy. If you don't have an enemy, you don't have anyone on which to project your shadow, and thus are forced to face yourself. It can be painful and difficult to look at ourselves. It always seems much easier to create a racial conflict or a war—at least, world events would suggest that this way of dealing with our shadows seems to be a more automatic response for most of us.

If we look at the opposing sides of social and political conflicts, we can often see what each group is trying to dis- own in itself. We see how those disowned parts are reflected by the other parties involved. For example, in a traditional patriarchal society, the masculine principle of rationality and order is celebrated while the intuitive, feeling, feminine principle is suppressed. This is reflected in the fact that men play a more dominant role, at least appearing to hold the power, while women are more subservient, oppressed or disempowered. This is an external reflection of what's hap- pening internally in each person; i.e., the masculine aspect within men is controlling and suppressing the feminine within them, often because it is a "mystery" that they fear and distrust.

Meanwhile, the women have an internalized, patriar- chal, masculine energy within them, who suppresses their feminine power and devalues them because they are women. In a strongly patriarchal society, most participants, both men and women, are consciously or unconsciously supporting that process.

As we—both men and women—have begun to bring our masculine and feminine energies into balance, integrating them internally, the external roles of men and women have been changing accordingly. As the external roles become more balanced, they support further internal balance. The internal and external processes reflect and support each other. However, as we move out of the old patriarchal men- tality and women begin to reclaim their own power, there is an initial tendency for many women to project their sup- pressed or denied, internal, dominating, patriarchal energy onto men in general and blame them for the woman's oppression. And many men deal with their fear of their own feminine energy by attempting to control women and keep them in subservient roles. As the process is evolving, however, more members of both sexes are gaining the ability to take responsibility for their own part in the process.

Some years ago, Sam Keen published a very interesting book which he called *Faces of the Enemy*. It was a collection of war posters and political cartoons, depicting the *faces of the enemy* in highly stylized, distorted forms. Keen showed how during a war or revolution the enemy is portrayed as a stereotype that shows very little variation and has very little to do with the actual characteristics of the society involved. In the cartoons and posters, a whole society was depicted as being all alike. Usually, the impression given was that the entire race or culture was subhuman and capable of the most inhuman acts.*

This is not to say that the qualities we dislike in ourselves don't also actually exist in people who are acting out those qualities in the external world. Most often they do. For example, Adolph Hitler was guilty of the most heinous of acts. However, the point is that until we learn to take responsibility for our own shadows, we will continue to project our denied aspects outside us—a process that actually empowers those people and forces which mirror them.

Sometimes an internal human conflict is played out in a particularly dramatic, intense, and often tragic way on the world stage. While such events can be extraordinarily painful, destructive, and horrifying, they can also be transformational, created on some level by the mass consciousness in order to wake ourselves up. The most extreme example of this in recent history—so gruesome that one hesitates to even try to discuss it in these terms—was the Holocaust. Hitler and the Nazis demonstrated the incredible extreme of the human tendency to blame, scapegoat, and victimize other people. In allowing this to take place, the German

---

* From the book by Sam Keen, *Faces of the Enemy*, published by Harper and Row, New York, 1986.

people, as well as those of us across the ocean who put off even denouncing Hitler's actions, acted out the tendency we all have to deny unpleasant realities and follow along with authority figures rather than risk a confrontation by speaking out or acting upon our own inner truth. And those who were persecuted revealed to all of us the ultimate horror that can be experienced through identifying with the victim aspect of our consciousness.

Of course, there is much more to it than we have the space to develop here, but it is also important to begin taking a look at all such human carnage as something that arises out of unhealed aspects of our collective consciousness. From a human perspective, all such events are numbingly horrifying and make absolutely no sense at all. From a larger perspective, however, it's perhaps possible to see them as a way that the collective consciousness dramatically acts out unconscious forces so that we can recognize, claim, and heal them. The impact of these experiences is so intense that the mass consciousness has to make a leap forward in its evolution. Of course, it takes time for these lessons to penetrate the consciousness of all cultures and individuals; hence we are still seeing plenty of terrible conflicts, many of them all too similar to the Holocaust, such as the so-called "ethnic cleansing" in the former Yugoslavia.

A very interesting example of internal polarities being played out on the world stage was the confrontation a few years ago between the United States, headed by George Bush, and Iraq, headed by Saddam Hussein. The United States has become very identified, at least in the minds of most Americans and our allies, with being the "good guys" —the ones who use our tremendous power in the world for good, justice, and peace. George Bush, very much identified with the good guy stance, represented "might for right" leadership.

The shadow side of the U.S., as mirrored in Saddam Hussein, has as its source the many political and economic forces and individuals within this country, that are motivated by *anything but* goodness, justice, and truth, but rather by greed and lust for power. Saddam Hussein is the perfect representative of this shadow side of ourselves. He unabashedly represented pure, self-serving aggression and the philosophy of "might makes right." Given the energies involved, perhaps we had to go to war with him. But in doing so, did we fail to recognize and own the reflection of our shadow?

One of the clearest and most obvious examples of how we project our disowned energies onto another group of people and then attempt to suppress those energies by oppressing the people who represent them to us, is in racial conflicts. It's interesting that throughout the world, people of lighter skin color tend to oppress darker skinned people—i.e., those who literally represent their shadow side. Darker skinned people, on some level, have apparently, down through history, bought into the belief system that they are somehow inferior; thus, their light-skinned external oppressors eventually come to represent, within their unconscious minds, "proof" that supports their own internalized oppressive belief structure. When they begin to rebel and fight back against the external power structure, they simultaneously (consciously or unconsciously) confront and fight their internal self-doubt and self-hatred, reclaiming their own power and self-respect. I believe that this was reflected in the slogan "Black is beautiful," which grew out of the victories of the Civil Rights movement of the '60s and '70s, and in its own way reflected a healing within the oppressed.

As I mentioned earlier in this book (see page 29), Deena Metzger gives a fascinating example of how she recognized the "political process" within her own psyche. This is excerpted from her excellent article, Personal Disarmament: Negotiation with the Inner Government:*

---

* Published in *Revision*, vol. 12, no. 4.

In a small, segregated country, called Zebra, the Sun minority has relegated the Shade majority to reservations far from the cities and the centers of power. Some Shades work for the Suns or are exhibited in the lavish national parks developed for the enjoyment of foreigners. The government is a theocracy, with a dictator who has allegiance to the oligarchy and priests.

The dictator, as well as the majority, knows nothing of the culture, mores, values, or spiritual inclinations of the Shades; nevertheless, fear and control of the Shades is behind every governmental decision. It is fully believed that if the Shades came near prominence or power, the entire way of being of the country would be altered. The minority does not fear for its lives; it fears for its way of life. To change this would be worse than death.

One day there is a serious power outage. The power lines have been cut. Up to this point, energy has been the major export of this country. The country is paralyzed. The Shades do not deny they cut the lines but assert that the power has always belonged to them . . .

Deena goes on to explain:

This scenario could describe conditions in any one of numerous countries. In fact, it is a description of my own inner state of being, a political description of the nation-state of my own psyche. I have come to understand that an individual is also a country, that one contains multiple selves who are governed as nations are governed, and that the problems and issues that afflict nations also afflict individuals. For most of my life, I have been completely unconscious of the real mode of government and the status of the beings within my territory . . .

Therefore, albeit unwillingly, slowly and painstak-
ingly, I began to dismantle the minority supremacist
government. I did this although the Suns insisted this
meant the end of progress and growth, that it meant
disaster... I came to understand that the system of
government that controlled me internally was similar
to the systems of government in the world... It was
heartbreaking to realize that all the work I'd done in
the world was undermined by the constant seepage of
contrary values from my inner being. I could not be a
democrat in the world or promote democracy while I
was a tyrant within... I couldn't hope to accomplish
change in the ouside world until I changed the inner
one...

When I lectured on Personal Disarmament at the
Peace Tent at the Non-Governmental Organizations,
Unitied Nations Conference on Women in Nairobi in
July 1985, I asked an audience of African, American
and European women who it was that ruled their inner
countries.

The majority painfully acknowledged that they
were ruled by tyrants. They agreed that nothing could
change in the world until they also altered their inner
conditions... It wasn't that we thought we needed to
stop efforts in the public world, but that there was
other urgent work, on the inner plane, which had to
be pursued simultaneously.

Important strides can be made through social, political,
legal and other types of external action, toward dealing with
the problems of racism, sexism, religious bigotry, poverty,
violence, and all the other ills that plague humanity. However, I don't believe that any of these problems can find
broad, lasting solutions, reaching the deepest levels of our
being, until we as individuals are able to confront,
acknowledge, and heal these ills at their source—within our

own psyches. It is here that we will find the roots of our own racism, sexism, homophobia, prejudice, blame, greed, inner poverty, and hunger for satisfaction. If we truly want to stop tyrannizing others, or being victims of others, we must learn how to confront and heal the inner forces that cause us to tyrannize and victimize ourselves. We must learn to love, respect and honor all aspects of ourselves. By building a foundation of self-love, self-respect, and integrating all aspects of ourselves, we can at last honestly respect, forgive and have compassion for all our fellow beings. It is here that we will find the key to transform the quality of life on our planet.

Of course, one of the most serious reflections that we all need to take in and deal with is the way we human beings are exploiting and polluting our natural environment and the very Earth we live on. To me, this seems to mirror our deep disconnection from our spiritual essence and the resulting loss of awareness of our relationship to the whole of existence. Our insensitivity and mistreatment of the natural world all around us reflects our denial of our inner nature. Our amazing disregard for the long-term results of our actions mirrors how out of touch we are with the rhythms and cycles of life.

As we do our inner healing work and reclaim our natural feelings and energies, we automatically become more aware and sensitive to the energies of the world around us. Through reconnecting with and honoring our spiritual being, we recognize the spirit in everyone and everything. We learn to live in attunement with that spirit, in harmony and in balance with the Earth.

EXERCISE

Reading the Reflections in Your Mirror

Think of a problem or an issue in your community that particularly concerns you. Ask yourself if there is any way it might reflect or relate to an issue or process within you. Imagine that all the players in the drama represent parts of yourself. What would need to happen for the issue to be resolved or healed? Here are some examples:

One man was concerned about crowded and inhuman conditions in prisons and the fact that prisoners are locked up and punished rather than being rehabilitated. He asked what part of himself was feeling imprisoned, what parts of him were jailers, and what part represented the society that condemned the imprisoned part. And then he asked himself how he might go about rehabilitating his own "inner prisoner."

One woman was especially worried about poverty and homelessness. She asked if there was a part of herself that felt homeless and impoverished. And she then asked how she could provide that part of herself with what she needed.

Another man was upset by the fact that the industrialized nations are using most of the world's resources, while the underdeveloped nations live in poverty. He asked what were the developed aspects of himself that were using most of his available resources, while other aspects languished? And he then asked how he could bring them into balance.

A woman found that she was angry at the fact that criminals often go unpunished while their victims suffered. She asked who, within herself, was "getting away with murder" while another part felt like a victim. And her question was, what would she need to do to stop the inner murdering and release herself from being a victim.

Most of us feel concerned about almost all of these problems. Whatever we feel *most* "emotionally charged" about in the external world, however, is usually most closely related to our personal issues.

In doing this exercise, please keep in mind that finding a correlation or synchronicity between your personal issues and world issues is *not* to imply that we are to blame for those issues. However, as we heal our personal conflicts we do contribute to healing world problems.

If you do not find any relationship between world problems and your own, or you feel confused about this exercise, simply let it go. Keep open to the possibility of an insight about it arising at some time in the future.

Consciousness
and Spirituality

Unconditional love is something that arises naturally when we can accept all our feelings and love all parts of us, including the parts that aren't unconditionally loving.

It has been tremendously helpful for me to understand the difference between consciousness and spirituality. Spirituality is one type of energy—the energy that links us to our deepest essential nature and to the universal source. Consciousness is the awareness of all of the energies within us. Thus, it is quite possible to follow a spiritual path that is not necessarily a consciousness path. That is, we could work on developing the spiritual dimension of our being, without necessarily developing the other aspects. We can become spiritually developed and totally identified with our "spiritual self." In this case, we would usually disown many other energies, especially the physical and emotional ones. That's why we see so many people who are very highly attuned spiritually, but may be completely out of balance in their physical and emotional lives.

Consciousness, on the other hand, involves developing and integrating all the many aspects of our being, including but not limited to the spiritual. The path of transcendence is a spiritual path, while the path of transformation is a consciousness path. Contacting and developing our spiritual nature is an important part of the consciousness journey but there are many other important parts as well. The path of transformation involves a powerful commitment to every level of growth.

One of my concerns about the New Age movement is its focus on transcendence rather than transformation. Many are hoping that by developing spiritually, they can rise above their problems and not have to face the challenge of integrating their spiritual and human natures. They feel comfortable and safe exploring the spiritual and mental realms, but hope to avoid the more painful or difficult emotional healing work. Of course, it is a perfectly legitimate option to choose a transcendent path, but it will not bring about profound healing and wholeness for the individual or for the world. And ironically, the peace of mind that so many people seek on the transcendent path cannot be fully achieved by focusing exclusively on that reality.

Fortunately, starting in the 1960s, the human potential movement has been integrating a variety of therapies, physical systems and spiritual practices. For example, at human potential centers such as Esalen Institute in California and The Open Center in New York City, it is not unusual to find classes being offered that include bodywork, meditation, yoga, intuition training, movement classes, recovery groups, and psychotherapeutic techniques. And the recovery movement, spearheaded by Alcoholics Anonymous, is having a powerful impact on the consciousness of the world today, applying the twelve-step process for profound healing in a variety of life issues that range from early abandonment to drug addiction.

What stops people from embarking on the transformational path? For many, it is simply a lack of knowledge. They aren't aware that such an opportunity exists, or perhaps they aren't sure how to go about finding it. Hopefully this book can provide a kind of trail map for this journey.

But lack of knowledge is not the only roadblock on the consciousness path. Another one is fear. We all fear the unknown, of course, and this particular journey certainly is unpredictable in many ways. That's why it is so important to cultivate a personal relationship with our inner guidance. Unless we feel some sense of a higher force working with us, it is simply too frightening to leave our familiar territory.

Many people are afraid of emotional healing work. There are so many misunderstandings and stereotypes about psychotherapy. Unfortunately, there are also many less than adequate or downright harmful therapists and healers, and many people who have had negative, disappointing or downright traumatic experiences with them. So it is extremely important to choose your helpers wisely and carefully.

I have found that most people are afraid that if they begin exploring deep feelings, they will get stuck there and never emerge. When feelings have been repressed and disowned, they feel very intense and powerful, and it is easy to feel that they might overwhelm us forever if we ever give them the opportunity.

However, the facts are quite different. If we move into our healing process at our own pace, without pushing ourselves and with the right support, it is not nearly as difficult as we might fear. Each of us has an internal mechanism that guides the pace of our journey. Once we allow ourselves to experience an emotion freely, we discover that rather than washing us away, the wave of feeling gradually subsides and leaves us with a deep sense of wonderful peace.

In my own healing process, as well as with thousands of others I have participated in and guided over the last fifteen years, I can say wholeheartedly that deep emotional healing is possible and is within the reach of anyone willing to make the commitment and follow through on it.

In New Age circles there is much talk about unconditional love. Many teachers urge their followers to practice
forgiveness, be non-judgmental, and love fully without conditions, and many sincere seekers are earnestly trying to follow these teachings. I have a problem with the way these
ideas are often presented. Of course, judgments are
unpleasant, separating, and uncomfortable for all concerned. Forgiveness is a powerful and healing force for both
the giver and the recipient. And there's nothing more blissful than giving and/or receiving unconditional love. However, there is a lot of confusion and misunderstanding about
these processes, and much of what is being taught is coming
from the transcendent rather than the transformative
approach.

Again, we must recognize the difference between our
spiritual essence and human personality. As spiritual
beings, we are always at one with universal love, which is
always unconditional and non-judgmental. The personality,
however, has the goal of learning to live in the physical
world and get our emotional needs met. On the personality
level, we are fundamentally concerned with protecting and
caring for the vulnerable child within us; our feelings of
love are entwined with our needs for safety, trust, and
intimacy. We have powerful defense mechanisms in our personalities that can close off our feelings of love when we
don't feel safe.

Rather than denying or trying to suppress these feelings
and reactions, we need to respect and appreciate the function of our human personality. It is not by nature unconditionally loving. Much healing can take place when we
recognize this as a given and are able to honor both our spiritual and our human nature.

When we feel judgmental, rather than denying those
feelings, we need to look deeply into them to discover what
is triggering them. Usually, we feel judgmental when we are
frustrated because we have not followed our own truth in

some way, or because we are having to confront another person who is reflecting one of our disowned selves back to us. So, instead of simply blocking ourselves from experiencing our judgmental feelings, we need to be attentive to the fact that our judgments can provide us with clues for what we need to look at in ourselves; ultimately, they are healing gifts. If we try to suppress or ignore the feelings, we miss the opportunity for learning and consciousness. Condemning ourselves for being judgmental is simply judging ourselves for being judgmental!

As for forgiveness, many people try to forgive too soon, allowing them to avoid feeling emotions they are afraid of. When we have been emotionally wounded, we may have many feelings, including hurt, fear, grief, withdrawal, anger, rage, and even the desire for revenge. If we can allow ourselves to acknowledge and freely experience all these emotions as they arise, without trying to "fix" or change anything, we will eventually arrive naturally at a feeling of forgiveness.

Forgiveness occurs when we have completed the learning process of a particular experience and are ready to release it and move on. If we rush to forgive before we are actually ready, we may short-circuit our own learning process, repress our other feelings, and miss an opportunity for greater healing. There is definitely an important place and time for rituals of forgiveness, but only when we know we aren't using forgiveness as a way to avoid other parts of the process.

The key to unconditional love is found in the love our spirit has for our personality. When we can tap into spirit, we can unconditionally love ourselves—including the parts of us that are angry, judgmental, needy, and selfish. Then we naturally feel compassion and acceptance toward others as well. We recognize in them the same human attributes that we have learned to love in ourselves. By loving and honoring our own personality in this way, we gain clear vision about other people's development on the personality level. We can maintain appropriate boundaries, making wise choices about who it's appropriate to get close to. At the same time, through our connection with our own divine essence, we naturally recognize and acknowledge the spiritual being in everyone else, even those with whom we know we must maintain some distance.

In recent years, with the recovery movement, many people have learned how to be loving even as they are setting boundaries and distancing themselves from loved ones who are having problems with addictive behavior. For example, they often have to learn that the most loving and compassionate act can be to confront the addictive person with the raw truth about how they are hurting other people. People who actually get through the recovery process generally attribute the beginning of their healing to having a loved one confront them in this way and insist that they get into a treatment program or support group.

Hal Bennett recently shared a story with me that perhaps helps to illustrate this point further. When he first graduated from college he got a job teaching a group of children with serious behavioral problems. After the first week of working with them, he was about to resign. He told his supervisor that the children were too violent with him and with each other. Indeed, each week there were runs to the emergency room to repair everything from bloody noses to broken arms. Hal's head teacher asked him to give it two more weeks and in that time he should keep two things in mind: First, that he could not succeed with these children until he learned how to love them, and second, that he would never learn to love them until he had accepted the fact that virtually any one of them was capable of stabbing him in the back if he didn't watch himself.

In the beginning this seemed like a contradiction. But after two weeks he had begun to see the wisdom in what his supervisor had said. Prior to their conversation, his judgments had rightly identified the children's behavior as violent and potentially dangerous to him and others. But there was a part of this labeling process that also created a huge wall between himself and the kids. In his mind, he had rejected them because of their behavior, telling himself that they were unworthy of his or anyone else's attention.

In the days that followed, he began meditating on what his supervisor had told him. He accepted the fact that the children were violent in their behavior, but he stopped seeing that behavior as a reason for rejecting them. He began to see a little beyond their outward actions, that within each of them was still a very tender, loving spirit. In order to get to that spirit, he had to find ways to deal with their violence — not deny it, but help them learn how relate to each other in more appropriate ways.

Learning to transform the violent behavior, which came from a very deep place of hurt and deprivation, required him to look at his own angry and violent feelings and begin healing them, too. He and the four other teachers assigned to these children worked together both to confront their own feelings and to seek more effective ways of creating a healing environment. Hal ended up staying at this school for another three years, and as part of a very dedicated teaching team helped to transform the lives of nearly thirty children.

◆ ◆ ◆

Remember that it doesn't really work to *try* to feel love, or any other feeling. Our feelings are not controlled by our will, and most attempts to assert this kind of power over them leads to denial, repression, and disowning parts of ourselves, or to an expression of feeling that is not authentic. By acknowledging and honoring any feeling — no matter how "unacceptable" we might have previously judged it to be — we create space for its opposite. So *trying* to love unconditionally is a contradiction. Unconditional love is something that arises naturally when we can accept all our feelings and love all parts of us, including the parts that aren't unconditionally loving.

MEDITATION

Accepting Ourselves and Others

Get in a comfortable position, lying down or sitting up with your back straight and supported. Take a few slow, deep breaths and let your body and mind relax into a quiet state of being. Ask to be in touch with the part of you that is judgmental. Ask it who or what it feels judgmental about and why. Ask how this judgment reflects on any parts of yourself which you don't accept.

Now ask to be in touch with the spiritual aspect of your being that is unconditionally loving. Ask that loving part of you if it can teach you how to accept all aspects of yourself, including your judgmental self and the parts of you that it rejects. Imagine a beautiful pink light of love and acceptance all around you. Now imagine looking at others with the compassion that you are gaining through accepting yourself.

MAKING A DIFFERENCE
IN THE WORLD

---

*As we clear out our spiritual, mental, emotional
and physical blocks and limitations, the creative
life force can move through us more fully and
freely. This life energy naturally moves us to
take action that is in harmony with our being,
in alignment with our higher purpose, necessary and effective in the world.*

I n my early youth, I was very involved in political and
social causes. I was raised in a politically active, liberal
family, and I was encouraged to express my views and take
action suporting the principles in which I believed. I wrote
letters to the editor of the newspaper; I wrote to my elected
representatives (although I was too young to vote); I volun-
teered in the local Head Start program, and I took part in
many demonstrations. My first month in college I was jailed
overnight for protesting the Vietnam war. I believed that I
could make a difference, and I was determined to do everything I could to make this world a better place.

Gradually a certain disillusionment crept in and took
over my experience. Politically, events were not encourag-
ing. The Kennedy and King assassinations, the defeat of
candidates and causes I believed in, the war dragging on ...

all these were very disheartening to me. When Nixon was elected to the Presidency, I gave up. Ironically, by the time I was old enough to vote, I didn't bother.

Much more profound than my political discouragement was the fact that I was going through a deep existential crisis, questioning the very meaning and purpose of my life. I felt vaguely empty, alone, dissatisfied; I wondered who I was and why I existed. My search for meaning and fulfillment opened me to the beginning of my consciousness journey.

For many years my focus was primarily inward, seeking to know and understand myself and the essential nature of life. Intuitively, I sensed that real changes and true satisfaction in life could only be found by addressing these core issues. I worked hard to know and develop myself on all levels — spiritual, mental, emotional, and physical. I went through a profound healing process that was sometimes painful and difficult, as well as fascinating and exciting. From the beginning, as I discovered helpful ideas and tools, and gradually gained wisdom, I found myself sharing what I was learning with others through counseling, leading workshops, and writing books.*

During all this time, I had very little interest in the external reality of the world. I seldom read newspapers or watched television, so I knew little about current events. I wasn't trying to avoid these things. I just didn't feel much connection with them. Although I knew I was part of the mass consciousness that created this world, I was more strongly focused on a different reality. It felt like I, and others who were on a consciousness path, were in the process of building a whole new world inside of ourselves. I was completely absorbed in the task of transforming my own awareness and creating a new reality, so I had very little energy for the old world around me.

---

* If you are interested in knowing more specifically about my life, I have shared my personal story in *Return to the Garden*.

My process, I believe, is quite typical of a great many people of my generation. It is a process that has been largely misunderstood and misinterpreted, especially by the media. I have read many newspaper and magazine articles lamenting the passing of the idealism and activism of the '60s and early '70s. If one were to believe these articles, that idealism and activism have all evaporated into nothingness. No doubt some people did abandon their beliefs, but for many of us, the process of radical change deepened. It did not fade at all but became more internal, more quiet and personal.

It has been very fashionable in the popular media, and even in the politically-oriented alternative media, to criticize any type of personal growth activities as "narcissistic and self-indulgent." While such criticism may be valid for certain individuals, it completely misses the mark in terms of what most of us on a consciousness journey have been doing. Rather than avoiding the external world, we have been laying the inner groundwork for outer change.

Here is my general view of the evolution of consciousness in this century:

In the first half of the century, most of the world was consumed by intense cataclysmic events—two world wars, a major economic depression, and mass genocide. These catalyzed tremendous growth for humanity, forcing us to face our darkest shadows and deepest fears, and compelling us to begin to see the world and humanity as one whole, interrelated system.

The '50s were an era of restabilization along with an effort to attempt to find order, balance, and some semblance of "normalcy." The late '50s and '60s brought a tremendous opening up to the non-rational forces of life—the instinctual, emotional, intuitive and spiritual—first through rhythm-and-blues and then rock-and-roll music, and later through psychedelic drugs. There was huge rebellion against the limits of the overly linear, logical, and controlled Western mind, and the corresponding social, political, and military power structure.

In the '70s, for the first time in Western history, a relatively large number of people were actually experiencing non-linear, transpersonal, and even mystical states of consciousness. This opened the way for many to seek spiritual understanding, healing practices, and alternative lifestyles. Many Westerners became fascinated with the wisdom of the East, and/or of the Earth-centered spirituality of indigenous peoples, such as our Native Americans.

In the '80s, many of us continued to deepen and expand our consciousness journeys. Much of our learning and growth came as we brought that process more into the world of form, through creating and nurturing careers and families. This was often painful and difficult. In the past, the vast majority of human beings lived in one geographical location, had one job, and stayed in one marriage for their entire lives. Finding that we could no longer do these things in the old ways, we've tried to discover new ways to live in the world, with few role models to guide us. Often feeling confused, and frequently feeling like failures in our attempts, we have nevertheless had the courage to keep risking.

Now, in the '90s, as we move rapidly toward the new millenium, the evolutionary process is gaining speed and intensity. The new world that we have been creating internally is being born, and the birth is not an easy one. We are undergoing a difficult labor! However, we are begining to see it take shape in the form of increasing numbers of people seeking social and political reform, and in increasing numbers seeking consciousness, not in order to escape the troubles of today's world but in order to take part in healing them.

Because this new world is emerging, the old one is dying and falling apart all around us. Old forms and institutions and systems simply aren't working anymore. To the degree that we are attached to that world—and it is difficult not to be—we feel frightened and confused. To the degree that we are already involved in the creation of the new, we feel elated and excited.

Many of us have a foot in both worlds and feel somewhat caught between realities, not quite knowing which to trust or believe in. We are frightened by the pain and chaos we see in the world. We're not sure how to handle our own personal life challenges. The problems of the world seem completely overwhelming. We'd like to do something to help, but we're not sure what to do.

Many of us who have been intensely focused primarily on an inner journey and/or the healing and development of our personal lives are feeling our energy begin to move outward again. All things move in cycles. Having gone deeply within, it is now time for many of us to begin to participate more openly and actively in the larger world. Synchronistically, this internal shift is being reflected by many things happening on our planet at this time. For one thing, our earthly environment seems to be deteriorating rapidly and we are growing increasingly concerned that we must tend to the problems immediately and effectively or it is going to be too late. Another factor is the changing political climate in the world and in our country.

When I first began getting ideas and writing notes for this book, the world was still visibly dominated by the old male, cold war mentality. It was still the Reagan/Bush era in this country, and the Soviet Union was still intact. There was a pervasive feeling of deadness and denial. I felt, however, that great change was happening, just under the surface, and I wanted to write a book that could help awaken people to that change and support those who were already at the forefront.

In the months since, as the book has been coming together, the atmosphere of the world has shifted considerably. The Soviet Union has dissolved, and the cold war is officially over. Many nations are undergoing massive change and "shake-ups" in their political and social structures. The United States has elected new leaders who represent a new generation, a different consciousness, and I believe a sincere desire to lead the country and the world in a different direction. Whether or not the new leaders will be able to accomplish their goals quickly and effectively is a more complex question. As always, in times of great change, there is the struggle between the old and the new mentalities, the status quo and the forces of change, with much fear, frustration and conflict, as well as hope and excitement.

It's interesting to look at these new leaders as reflections of the masculine and feminine energies within each of us. George and Barbara Bush represented the old patriarchal order, in which there is a pronounced split between male and female roles. George Bush is the designated leader, decision-maker, and wielder of external power; Barbara Bush is very much the quiet, supportive helpmate who uses her power in a more private, perhaps indirect way. By contrast, Bill and Hillary Clinton represent a strong shift in the direction of more balance and integration between the internal masculine and feminine energies. He seems very much in touch with his feminine side, honoring and valuing it, which is reflected in how he clearly respects and honors his wife's power. She, in turn, supports her inner feminine energies with a strongly developed masculine energy of her own, apparently comfortable with either leading or following. A more equal male-female partnership in the White House is, I believe, a reflection of a more balanced male-female partnership that we are developing within ourselves individually and culturally.

The inner consciousness work we have been doing is finally becoming manifest in a more visible way in this new worldwide atmosphere of change and transformation. These are exciting times; we are beginning to see the results of much hard work. It is only a beginning; there is tremendous chaos, struggle, and frustration around the process of change. But it is difficult to deny that it is happening.

For many of us on a consciousness journey, this atmostphere of change is re-igniting our hope and our vision, inspiring us to get involved in the world in some more active way. Yet, these feelings may generate new inner conflicts. Expecially for those who have been following a transcendent spiritual path, there may be tremendous contradictions to be faced between separating ourselves from worldly involvement and plunging into the middle of things. How do we become involved in the external world without losing the internal connection we're worked so hard to achieve?

Just as the world is at a great turning point, so is the consciousness movement. Rather than following a transcendent path and withdrawing from the world, we must commit ourselves to the transformational path and take responsibility for changing the world.

We must remember that trying to solve the world's problems through a primarily external focus is not very effective, either. The world is full of people attempting to find solutions to community and planetary problems with little success and much struggle, because they are not fully contronting deeper levels of the issues. As well-meaning as we may be, if we try to "fix" things outside ourselves, without healing the underlying causes of the problem in our own consciousness, we simply perpetuate the problem.

For example, in recent years there have been many gatherings to visualize world peace. I am, as many know, a great believer in the power of visualization, having written the book, *Creative Visualization*, many years ago. So I encourage people to continue to use this powerful tool for achieving personal and collective goals. However, visualizing world peace or anything else will only be effective if we are willing to do the personal consciousness work that will support it. If we are identified with love, light, and peaceful energies, and we project our disowned aggression onto others, our attempts to create world peace, or even peaceful lives of our own, will most likely fail. If we are able to own our natural aggression in a healthy way, claiming our inner warrior as the important part of us that he is, and making him a part of our lives, then aggression wll not be a shadow that we project onto others. The masters of Eastern martial arts understand this principle—that if you are at peace with, and you know how to channel the energy of your inner warrior, that power will radiate from you and you will most likely never need to be overtly aggressive.

The fact that disowning our aggression does not ultimately lead to peace is illustrated in the death of Mohandas Gandhi. Gandhi himself was completely committed to nonviolence and did much incredible work in the world. Tragically, his own life ended violently; his assassin may have reflected Gandhi's disowned aggressive shadow side which turned against him. John Lennon is another example. He was apparently aggressive and even violent as a young man. In later life he disowned that side of himself and tried to promote world peace. He, too, died tragically and violently, still a young man. And it is my belief that, like Gandhi's assassin, Lennon's assassin reflected Lennon's own unresolved aggression.

Ultimately, if we want to live peaceful lives and create a peaceful world, we must start by building the foundation for that peace within ourselves. This process includes accepting and integrating the parts of ourselves that are capable of making war.

So how can we fulfill our desire to actively make a difference in the world? We must discover how to take action that is a natural extension of our consciousness process. These actions can only be effective if they are firmly rooted in the soil of our inner healing work—everything that I have been describing in this book.

First, we must understand that we are all truly part of one whole, that all of creation is, at the deepest level, one consciousness, one intelligence. Therefore, we must remind ourselves that *everything* we do has meaning and significance; to some degree, *all* our actions affect everyone. We must do our inner work with the knowledge that in healing ourselves we contribute to healing everyone and everything. It's fairly easy to see that we affect the people we personally encounter, and to understand that they in turn affect the people with whom they interact, so that our influence spreads out into the world through every personal contact. We may need to make a leap of faith to grasp that through the collective consciousness—in which we are all active participants—we also affect people on the other side of the world. We affect each other though we may never have any personal contact.

I believe that everyone on the planet who is involved in a personal growth process is part of the "healing generation." It is our destiny to do a tremendous amount of inner work so that the generations that follow us will not have so much healing to do and can thus get on with whatever work they come here to accomplish! So, for many of us, it may very well be that the inner work we do will be our greatest contribution to humanity.

Certainly, if we want our external actions to be as powerful and effective as possible, we need to be deeply committed to our ongoing, ever-deepening consciousness journey. We need to remember to use every important relationship, every significant experience we have, as a mirror, providing us with reflections that help us continue to learn how we can express more of our potential and live more consciously.

Everything we think, feel, say and do has some affect on other people and the world around us. Therefore, the most powerful and important thing we can do to change the world is simply to do our best to live a conscious life on a daily basis. Remember, this does not mean living up to some lofty spiritual ideal—always being unconditionally loving, accepting and forgiving. Trying too hard to conform to *any* model of perfection, no matter how appealing it might be, will always lead to disappointment and feelings of failure. We don't have to be saints before we can start making a difference!

To me, living consciously means accepting our human weaknesses and imperfections without judging ourselves harshly, and being willing to learn from our unconscious patterns of behavior once we become aware of them. It means looking at our experiences as gifts that can help us grow, recognizing everyone and everything we encounter as a potential teacher. It means taking responsibility (not blame) for our thoughts, feelings, and actions, recognizing that they do have an effect on others. It means listening and reaching deeply inside ourselves to find our inner sense of truth, then doing our best to speak and live that truth moment to moment and day by day. And it means generously sharing the gift of our being, as well as our special talents and abilities, with others.

To live consciously we need to reclaim and develop our awareness of how we live on the earth. Most of us need to learn to live more simply, without using up so many resources and creating so much waste. This does not mean that we need to live in poverty or suffer feelings of deprivation and scarcity. Quite the contrary! As we become aware of our *real* needs—spiritually, mentally, emotionally and physically—and as we learn to truly fulfill these needs, we will find we have less need for much of the external stuff that we're using to try to fill our emptiness. As true needs are filled, false needs dissolve, along with the fears that have driven us. As we are filled from within with our own spirit, and as our life force moves more freely through our bodies, as we move into alignment with our souls and our higher purpose, we feel a part of the natural flow and abundance of the universe. We come to appreciate the wealth in life's simpler things.

This doesn't mean we can't enjoy our material possessions and the products of our remarkable technology. I believe that when we are in balance with ourselves, we will find a harmonious way to balance the needs of our environment, along with enjoying the fruits of our material creativity. Meanwhile, most of us need to develop more awareness and better habits in the use of our resources. The little things matter—such things as buying healthier and more natural foods, with less packaging, fewer chemical additives and less processing, avoiding products that are toxic or which come in non-recyclable containers, carrying along your own canvas bag when shopping, recycling at home and at the office. All of these can seem like small things, but each one can make a big difference, especially as we teach our children these practices.

Another important part of living consciously, of course, is how we treat our fellow humans, not to mention our animal friends, on a daily basis. Of course, we all say and do things that we later regret and feel bad about. That is an unavoidable part of being human, *especially* when we are actively engaged in learning new ways of living and relating, rather than following the safe path we may have found in the past. So we need to allow ourselves plenty of room to express ourselves in ways that may not always turn out to be harmonious or successful. However, we can also make an extra effort, when we are able, to share our love and caring with others, in small ways, such as making eye contact and saying a real thank you to the tolltaker on the bridge, or having a little extra patience with a store clerk who's obviously having a difficult day.

Living consciously means living creatively, looking at each new day not only as an opportunity to learn but also as an opportunity to enjoy sharing our special gifts, talents and inspirations, in small and large ways.

As we do our inner healing work, we automatically tap into more and more of our own natural creative energy. As we clear out our spiritual, mental, emotional and physical blocks and limitations, the creative life force can move through us more fully and freely. This life energy naturally moves us to take action that is in harmony with our being, in alignment with our higher purpose, necessary and effective in the world.

By following your creative ideas and impulses, you may find yourself doing unusual and unexpected things, some of which may develop in interesting ways. For example, a friend of mind who is a composer had created the music for a film on ecology. When the film played in the local community, he had the impulse to buy tickets for all his friends to go and see it, in order to help raise their consciousness about the topic. The event truly did help them to become more aware of and caring about the environment. Everyone who went was so inspired that they got together to brainstorm some ways to get the film better exposure. They purchased copies of the film on video and took it around to different school districts for all the children to see.

While no single person felt that it had taken a huge amount of time, energy or money to do what they did, their efforts did make a tremendous difference in the world, spreading a message that was important and healing.

Here are some guidelines that may help you discover how to take "right action:"

◆ Make a commitment to yourself to discover meaningful and effective action that you can take to contribute to and support healing and transformation in the world. Look around you to see some of the problems and issues in your immediate environment or out in your community.

◆ When you find yourself attracted to an issue you would like to help heal in the external world, ask yourself if there is anything you need to do first on an *inner* level. How might this problem reflect an issue within your own psyche, and what do you need to do to resolve that issue within yourself? If you don't get an answer or see any clear correlation, don't worry. Let it go, but keep the question open as you proceed. At some point you may have a further insight about this.

◆ Ask your inner guidance for clarity and direction regarding any kind of action you are thinking about taking. If no inner guidance comes, let it go for awhile. Something may come up later. If nothing does, this may not be an area where you are meant to take action. Instead, notice where you *do* have energy to do something.

◆ When you feel an impulse in a certain direction, follow it. Continue to ask for guidance and follow it as best you can. When you don't feel clear about your direction, rest.

◆ Don't bite off more than you can chew or be too ambitious in your plans. Take small steps and remember that the little things can count as much as the big ones.

◆ Do what you genuinely have energy to do. Try not to act out of guilt or fear. As much as possible, follow your inspiration. Do what is exciting, enlivening and/or personally satisfying to you.

For example, a woman I know read an article in the newspaper telling how the local school district, for financial reasons, had to cut its after school program of arts classes for young people. She felt distressed by this because when she was a child a similar after school class had led her to her lifelong love of dance and theater. She asked her inner guidance to let her know if there was something she could do to help. A few days later she had a strong feeling to call the school district and volunteer her help. She ended up teaching after-school theater classes for several years and absolutely loved her experience with the children.

Many of the things we are guided to do in our lives may not *seem* to have a direct connection with helping anyone or healing the world. Remember that the greatest contribution that you can make is in the aliveness that comes from simply being yourself, living your truth, and doing what you love. The passionate expression of who we are will heal the world.

SEVEN STEPS
ON THE PATH
OF TRANSFORMATION

Remember that healing doesn't happen over-night—it's an ongoing process. Often it may be uncomfortable, at times painful, but there are few ventures in life that are more fascinating and rewarding. Trust your own process and give it time and space to unfold on its own way.

Some readers may be just beginning their consciousness process. Others may have been doing this work for years, yet reading this book has perhaps given them a new insight or a different perspective.

For those who are wishing to consciously begin or renew your transformational journey, here are seven fundamental steps:

1. Making a Commitment

Make a conscious commitment to yourself to follow your truth as best you can, and to do whatever it takes to learn, grow, heal and gain awareness. You may want to do this privately, or with your partner, family, friends or a group. If you wish, make a statement of commitment and create a ritual to formalize the event for yourself: write it in your journal, do a meditation in a special place, walk on the beach and shout it to the ocean, find a power object that symbolizes the step you are taking and keep it with you or create a personal altar of special objects, wear a special ring or other piece of jewelry, create a work of art that expresses your feelings about this step, or anything else that feels right for you.

2. Following Inner Guidance

Develop a relationship with your own inner teacher by practicing the art of listening to and following your inner intuitive guidance. I have described this in chapters on "Finding Your Inner Teacher" and "Developing Inner Guidance."

3. Finding Support

Reach out for the support you need for your journey. Many of us have the idea that we must be totally self-sufficient, making changes in our lives without assistance from anyone. We may feel that it is somehow shameful or embarrassing to admit we need help. The fear of acknowledging our vulnerability in this way is one of the old limiting patterns that we need to heal. As human beings we do need each other. We are a socially oriented species, and we need to have a feeling of belonging within a family, group, or community. And the consciousness process is far too complex and difficult to manage alone. Of course there are times when we need to face being alone, turning inward for answers and trusting our own sense of self rather than looking to others. Learning to discern when we need support and when we need to be independent is all part of the process.

For you, support may be in the form of a good friend or group of friends, your partner and/or family, a mentor or a trusted adviser, a doctor or healing practitioner, a counselor or therapist, a teacher, a class, a professional organization, a church or spiritual group, a workshop, a therapy group, a recovery group or twelve-step program.

Be careful and selective when choosing your support systems. Make certain they really address and satisfy your own specific needs. A good rule of thumb is that generally you should come away from the experience feeling better about yourself, feeling empowered, enlivened, or more at peace. Of course there may be times when you feel differently—shaken or disturbed because an old pattern is being challenged, perhaps. But overall, the feeling should be a positive one for you. Beware of any situation where you frequently feel belittled, criticized, confused, frustrated, or disempowered. This may indicate that someone is on a power trip. Be particularly cautious if they tell you it's for your own good, or say that you are being resistant if you question their techniques.

We all need at least one person or group with whom we can be fully ourselves, where we can feel safe to share our innermost thoughts and deepest feelings, where we feel accepted for who we are, including the qualities we might consider our flaws or weaknesses. Aside from this basic support, we may also require more specific kinds: the need for inspiration, the need for help in learning skills, or the need for help from a health practitioner. A support person can be any friend or specialist who assists you on the transformational path, either directly or indirectly.

The type of support you need will probably vary from time to time. Sometimes we outgrow our support people and when we do it can be difficult to let go of them, even when we recognize that it is time to do so. Sometimes it is vital to let go and move on. Again, knowing when to stay and when to go is a wisdom that is only gained by meeting the challenge when it comes up in your life.

Keep in mind, too, that as wonderful as our friends and family may be, there are times when we need support from a more objective source. Our loved ones have their own attachments and investments in our lives and can't always offer us the perspective we need. Also, they may not have the skills or expertise we need in a given area. And expecting all our needs for emotional support to be met by our spouse, partner, family, or closest friends may simply be too great a burden on them, especially when we're going through an emotional crisis or deep healing. Getting outside or professional guidance at these times can be crucial to our own well-being as well as the well-being of our loved ones.

When seeking support, get as clear as you can about what you need. This doesn't mean that you have to know exactly what you need; just get in touch with whatever you *are* aware of and go from there. For example, you may realize that you need to learn to communicate better in relationships, but not be sure exactly what that would look like, or what skills you need. Ask for inner guidance to direct you toward appropriate support. Ask friends and acquaintances for recommendations and referrals. Consult any other sources you can think of. When you find something that sounds interesting or feels appropriate, check it out. Don't be afraid to interview a potential adviser, healer, or therapist to see how you feel about them and how you work together. Most therapists offer an initial session to interview each other. It is often a good idea to start out on a trial basis. Above all, trust your gut feelings about what's right for you, and keep following your inner guidance.

4. Using Tools

Find tools that can help you with your process on all four levels—spiritual, mental, emotional, and physical. Allow yourself to explore, investigate, and discover different ideas, techniques, and practices that attract your interest to find out what works best for you at any given time. When you are in an exploratory phase, you may read books, listen to tapes, or watch videos on various topics, take classes, consult with experts or advisers until you find a skill or method that works for you. Then you may find yourself concentrating on a particular practice or two for awhile. Again, remember that your needs change as you grow; tools that you once used regularly may be placed on the shelf for awhile or discarded altogether as you find new ones. You may also find that there is a time for letting go of all tools for growth, and just allow yourself to *be* for awhile!

Some of the tools that have been most important in my process over the years are (more or less in the order in which they came into my life): dance, hatha yoga, meditation, the idea that we create our own reality, the techniques of creative visualization and affirmation, contacting and clearing core beliefs, many different kinds of emotional release work and therapeutic modalities, massage and body work, the practice of trusting and following inner guidance, balancing male and female energies, twelve-step work with co-dependency issues, the psychology of selves, and voice dialogue. There have been many others as well. I mention these not to endorse them specifically, but to give you an idea of the range of different tools that have helped me at various times — and still are helping me.

5. Allowing Healing

Make consciousness growth a high priority in your life. Create time and space to allow your healing process to occur on all levels. Regardless of the type of support you've created or the tools you have chosen, the basic healing process involves gaining insight and awareness about yourself, learning to accept and be comfortable with all aspects of yourself, learning to trust, care for, and love yourself.

Because of the unconsciousness and denial that exists on the planet today, we have all been wounded to some degree. Some, of course, have suffered more than others, and therefore may need to spend more of their time and energy healing. Try not to compare your process with anyone else's. We all have our own journey to make and each one is different, depending on the lessons we came into this life to learn and the gifts we came to give—wherever the deepest pain exists, that's where there will be the greatest learning. And there also you will find much that you will have to share with others.

Remember that healing doesn't happen overnight—it's an ongoing process. Often it may be uncomfortable, at times painful, but there are few ventures in life that are more fascinating and rewarding. Trust your own process and give it time and space to unfold on its own way.

6. Expressing Creativity

Discover ways to express your creativity. Everyone is naturally creative, and expressing our creativity is an important part of finding wholeness and fulfillment. In fact, the inability to express our natural creative energy is a root cause of many addictions, as well as our spiritual, mental, emotional, and physical pain. The more healing we experience on all levels, the more our creativity begins to emerge.

If you feel your creativity has been blocked, you may need to do some emotional healing, specifically in this area. Get some support to help you discover how and why it got stopped or suppressed, and what is standing in the way of letting it flow.

Getting in touch with and healing your inner child may be a key for unlocking your creativity. Young children are endlessly creative because they have not yet become inhibited. Our creativity often gets dampened or smothered once we begin to develop the inner *perfectionist* and *critic*. Our perfectionist tells us how things should be done and sets very high standards for us. Our inner critic points out every time we fall short of perfection. (Being human, this is most of the time!) This can make us unwilling to try new things or express ourselves for fear that we won't do it well enough. We may need to do some conscious healing work with our inner critic and perfectionist, who are actually just trying to protect us from external criticism by trying to shape us up to be as perfect as possible. Keeping their best intentions in mind, it can be a good idea to get them to relax a little bit. Then it becomes much easier to contact the naturally spontaneous child within us and encourage him/her to start expressing more in our lives.

To encourage our own creativity we need to lighten up a little bit, have some fun, be adventurous. We need to take some risks to express ourselves in new and different ways. Take small steps first. Try some things that seem fun and creative to you—draw a picture, build something, take a cooking class, an art, dance, or martial arts class, take up a musical instrument, join an amateur theater group, take up a sport, write a poem or short story, plant a garden. Do it strictly for your own enjoyment, not for anyone else's approval. The purpose of our creativity is our own fulfillment; the goal is not to please other people or win their approval.

Remember that creativity expresses itself in many ways and each person has his or her own unique way. You may express your creativity primarily through your work, through raising your children, through a favorite hobby, through remodeling or decorating your home, through the way you dress, or gardening, or cooking, or healing.

7. Sharing with Others

Passing on to others what we have received and learned is an important part of completing that process at each level of our healing and growth. We have not fully integrated anything until we have manifested it in our experience in a way that impacts others in some transformational way.

However, this is not something we have to try to do. It simply happens automatically as we follow the other six steps. Primarily it happens on an energetic level. The more inner healing we accomplish, the more life force can move through our bodies. This life energy has an impact on everyone we encounter, regardless of our words or actions. The universe literally flows through us to "knock people alive," to awaken or speed up their transformational process. As we become more conscious, we influence the mass consciousness to shift, which then affects everyone's reality.

In a more obvious and specific way, as we express our creativity more fully and freely in our work and through our other interest, we make a contribution to others. Many of us may be drawn toward some form of consciousness or healing work, wishing to pass on to others the support and tools that have been so valuable to us. This is extremely rewarding and fulfilling, and the reflection we receive from the people we work with definitely helps us integrate our own consciousness process even more deeply. Also, as many have discovered, serving others can be one of the greatest highs available on the planet!

However, it doesn't really matter what our specific activities are. If our talent and our joy lies in repairing automobiles, studying an obscure insect species in a remote forest, selling computers, or baby-sitting children, and we do it with love and integrity, we will have a healing effect on everyone we encounter and the Earth itself.

Seven Steps
on the Path
of Transformation

1. Making a Commitment
2. Following Inner Guidance
3. Finding Support
4. Using Tools
5. Allowing Healing
6. Expressing Creativity
7. Sharing with Others

FULFILLING
OUR HIGHER PURPOSE

Our higher purpose is what we came here on a soul level to do. We are born with the specific interests, talents, and abilities to fulfill that purpose.

E very one of us comes into this life with lessons to learn and gifts to give. The more we learn and grow, the more we become capable of developing and sharing these natural gifts.

As we follow the seven steps on the path of transformation, outlined in the previous chapter, we find ourselves guided toward discovering and fulfilling our higher purpose in life. That higher purpose is, quite literally, the sharing of our gift.

Our higher purpose is what we came here on a soul level to do. We are born with the specific interests, talents, and abilities to fulfill that purpose. In fact, as we come into life we most likely choose the family and environment that will give us the exact combination of support, and challenges to overcome, that we most need to effectively accomplish our goals. Some of us choose more support in our early life, others choose environments of physical, emotional, mental and/or spiritual challenge! Regardless of the environment we've come from, if we can successfully reap the knowledge that is available in them, we are well on our way to recognizing and expressing our higher purpose.

Chances are that our higher purpose is already showing itself in our lives. It is usually there from the very beginning, expressing itself through who we are even as children. Whatever things we do naturally and easily, whatever our innate talents and interests, whatever knowledge and skills we've been led to develop, and whatever people and activities we are drawn to, all these provide us with clues about our higher purpose. We may already be expressing that purpose so naturally and easily that it's just no big deal. If so, we will have a feeling of fulfillment and contentment where that aspect of our lives is concerned.

Many of us have yet to discover our higher purpose, in which case there will probably be a sense of dissatisfaction and restlessness until we do. It has often been said that we ourselves are most blind to our greatest gifts. Many times, it is our friends and loved ones who see them most clearly. Often, these gifts, which others value so highly in us, are things that come very easily and perhaps even automatically to us. Part of what makes them so difficult for us to recognize is that they are associated with things that we find easy, enjoyable and effortless for us to do.

It is through these gifts that we can get in touch with our higher purpose. To do this, first think about a close friend. Since we are mirrors to each other, bring them into your mind and ask them first, what they value in you. What do you bring to their life that they feel improves it? You might even ask them, what is it in me that reflects the very best in you?

The answers you get may seem very modest or commonplace at first, but try not to underestimate their importance. In fact, after you've begun to get in touch with your gifts, start looking for ways that you might use them in a more conscious way. For example, one client, a woman I'll call

Lorna, found that what her closest friends valued most in her was her ability to listen to others in a way that they found both calming and empowering. Lorna herself had never thought of this as being a special gift since it was something that came to her so naturally. However, over the next few days she began to be more aware of the ways that her listening did, in fact, seem to give people encouragement, giving them the courage they needed to solve problems they were having or to go forward with plans when they were procrastinating.

The more conscious Lorna became of this gift, the more she saw it as an expression of a higher purpose. The last I spoke with her, she was exploring all the ways that she might express her talents professionally. Her choices at that time included taking a job with a company that teaches communication skills to going back to school to earn the necessary degrees to become a psychotherapist. Both these paths promised to make good use of her natural abilitites.

I recently saw a delightful story on the television news. They were doing a special "human interest" feature about a man who drives a street-sweeping machine. It seems that from earliest childhood, he had a great fascination with street sweepers! His mother showed pictures he had drawn and models he had made of them when he was a boy. Now he owns his own machine, and simply loves driving it for a living. This man was very warmhearted, friendly, and obviously enjoying his life tremendously. He seemed to be radiating wonderful energy everywhere he went. One would not normally think of driving a street sweeper as fulfilling one's higher purpose, but clearly this man was doing so!

As I mentioned earlier in the book, when I was a child I used to read and write stories all the time. I used to imagine that some day I would walk into a library and there would be a whole shelf full of books written by me! At the time, I was really into books about horses and other animals, so I thought that's what I probably would be writing.

Years went by, and I forgot all about this vision, and never wrote a thing. It wasn't until I had written and published my first book, *Creative Visualization*, that I remembered my childhood dream of being a writer. I've now learned, of course, that writing and teaching about consciousness is a major part of my higher purpose. This is not something I ever planned or decided to do. It evolved naturally out of my process, and out of who I am as a being. I teach and write because I am compelled to, for my own learning, as well as to share my gifts with others. It's something I can't *not* do!

If you don't feel that you are in touch with your higher purpose and you would like to be, ask your inner guidance to begin to bring you information, awareness, and clarity about it. Ask yourself what things you most enjoy doing, or just seem to find yourself doing frequently. How do you express yourself most easily and naturally? What fantasies did you have as a child? What are your fantasies and visions for yourself now? Spend some time exploring them.

Don't expect immediate answers to these questions. Be patient with yourself. The process of discovering and fulfilling your higher purpose may take years. It cannot be forced or rushed, since it is all part of your unfolding journey. Allow yourself to be with the questions without demanding answers. When answers do come, they may come in surprising ways and unexpected moments. Keep in mind that doing your consciousness work will automatically bring your higher purpose into focus and clarity over time.

Remember that your higher purpose is not just what you do. It is also who you are—your unique combination of energy, personality and physical form brings something special into the world. Keep in mind that you have never seen anyone with the same higher purpose as yours, since yours is unique! Your higher purpose has not been invented until you manifest it.

As Martha Graham has expressed:

There is vitality, a life force, an energy, a quickening that is translated through you into action. And because there is only one you in all time, this expression is unique. And if you block it, it will never exist through any other medium... the world will not have it. It is not your business to determine how good it is, nor how valuable, nor how it compares with other expressions. It is your business to keep it yours clearly and directly, to keep the channel open.*

---

* Agnes DeMille, *Dance to the Piper*, Atlantic Monthly Press, 1952.

ENVISIONING
THE FUTURE TOGETHER

For a long time, I felt deeply troubled both by the difficulties I was experiencing in my own personal life and by the pain and suffering I saw in the world. Through many years of consciousness work, I had developed a strong connection with my spiritual self. From that perspective I could see the perfection of the whole process; I had a strong faith that there was a meaning and purpose in it all, and that it would all work out well eventually. The human part of me felt more unsure; on the emotional level I had fears and doubts about my own future and the future of the planet. I wondered if my own personal needs would ever get fulfilled, much less the needs of all the beings on this Earth.

As my healing process has deepened and continued, I've found a great deal more integration within myself. This is being reflected as my life is gradually becoming more balanced and satisfying. Some of my most difficult patterns are slowly dissolving and I'm finding new ways to live my life that work better. Many of my deepest heart's desires are being fulfilled. Do I get stuck and feel frustrated? Yes, frequently! But not as profoundly or as lengthily as before. Watching my life, and the lives of many others near and dear to me, unfold in amazing ways has deepened my confidence that the principles I have been living and teaching really do work.

Along with my own healing has come a stronger sense of trust in the healing process going on in our world. Before, I wasn't quite sure whether we would actually be able to effect change quickly enough, or whether we would simply have to move onto another level of existence to continue our journeys.

I still feel pangs of fear and doubt sometimes when I am forced to confront some of the more upsetting aspects of our current reality. I expect that many external circumstances may get worse as the old order crumbles. Yet deep inside, I feel more strongly than ever before that we are participants in an amazing transformational process that is taking place here on Earth. I believe that we will succeed at our task, and that many of us will see results manifested in form within our lifetimes.

So I'd like to invite you to join me and all the other readers of this book in envisioning the future. Just as at the beginning of the book, I'm going to ask you to close your eyes and imagine the future. This time I'd like you to pay special attention to your most creative fantasies. If doubts and fears come, acknowledge them and allow them to be there, too. Then turn your attention to developing your vision. Don't limit it in any way. Allow it to be as expansive as you would like.

Get in a comfortable position with your pen and paper, journal, crayons, or whatever tools you'd like within easy reach. Close your eyes, and take a few slow, deep breaths. Let your awareness move into a quiet place deep inside of you. Ask yourself, "What is my vision of the future?"

First, focus your attention on imagining your own personal future as you would most like it to be. If you're not quiet sure how you want it to be, just allow yourself to go with one fantasy about it, knowing that you can change it whenever you want to. Imagine your relationship with yourself as fulfilling as possible on all levels—spiritual, mental, emotional, and physical. Imagine everything in your life reflecting the balance and harmony within your own being—your relationships, your work, your finances, your living situation, your creative pursuits. Allow them all to be wonderfully successful and satisfying.

Now expand your focus to imagine the future of the world around you—your community, your country, humanity, the natural environment, our planet. Allow them *all* to reflect the integration and wholeness you have found within yourself. Imagine the new world emerging and developing in a healthy, balanced, expansive way. Really let your imagination soar. Envision the world as you would love it to be, a paradise on Earth.

When you feel complete with this process, open your eyes. If you wish, write or draw your vision.

Thank you for joining me. Bless you.

APPENDIX:
RELAXATION EXERCISE

This exercise is designed for very deep relaxation. Just as with learning any kind of new activity, such as riding a bicycle or running, it takes awhile to train your body and mind to respond in a new way. The instructions given here will help you achieve a balanced and effective relaxation response in a minimum of time. Once you have done this longer version a few times, you'll discover that you can enter a deeply relaxed state within just a few seconds by closing your eyes and taking a few deep breaths.

Most people find that conscious relaxation of this kind is greatly enhanced by playing very soft, relaxing music in the background.

First give yourself permission to take five to ten minutes to relax deeply, without having to think about other things you should be doing. Choose a quiet place and time of day when this will be possible.

- ◆ Loosen any tight clothing.

- ◆ Sit in an alert, upright position, hands gently resting in your lap with your palms open.

- ◆ Take a deep breath and exhale slowly, allowing your shoulders to be loose and relaxed.

◆ Open your mouth wide. Yawn, or pretend you are yawning.

◆ Let the areas around your eyes and forehead be relaxed and loose. Let the areas around your nose, mouth and jaw be relaxed.

◆ Breathe slowly and easily.

◆ If ideas or feelings come into your mind at this time, pretend they are a telephone ringing in the distance, perhaps in a neighbor's house. You acknowledge that "someone is calling" but you do not have to answer.

◆ Take a deep breath, inhaling gently and slowly, imagining the breath entering your right nostril. Hold the breath for a moment, then exhale slowly and comfortably, imagining that you are exhaling through your left nostril.

◆ Take another deep breath, this time imagining your breath enthering your left nostril and exiting your right.

◆ Focus your attention on how your breath feels: cooling, as it enters your nostrils, perhaps gently expanding your chest as it fills your lungs, then slightly warming your nostrils as you exhale. You may wish to visualize the air as having a beautiful, vibrant color as it enters and exits your body.

◆ Repeat this breathing pattern until you have done at least four full cycles. A full cycle is one inhalation and one exhalation.

◆ With each cycle, focus your attention on one area of your body:

Be aware of your chest relaxing.
Be aware of your upper back relaxing.
Be aware of you arms and hands relaxing.

Be aware of your abdomen relaxing.
Be aware of your buttocks relaxing.
Be aware of your legs relaxing.
Be aware of your feet relaxing.

◆ Now let your breathing pattern return to normal as you enjoy the relaxed state you have created.

For several weeks, practice this relaxation exercise whenever the opportunity arises or whenever you feel a need to unwind and rest at work, at home or in your recreational life.

Recommended Resources

Books:

Bodine, Echo. *Passion to Heal: The Ultimate Guide to Your Healing Journey.* (Mill Valley, CA: Nataraj Publishing, 1993).

Capacchione, Lucia. *The Power of Your Other Hand: A Course in Channeling the Inner Wisdom of the Right Brain.* (North Hollywood, CA: Newcastle Publishing Co., Inc., 1988).

Capacchione, Lucia. *Recovery of Your Inner Child.* (New York: Simon and Schuster, 1991).

Gawain, Shakti. *Creative Visualization.* (San Rafael, CA: New World Library, 1978).

Gawain, Shakti (with Laurel King). *Living in the Light: A Guide to Personal and Planetary Transformation.* (Mill Valley, CA: Nataraj Publishing, 1993; originally published by New World Library, 1986).

Gawain, Shakti. *Return to the Garden: A Journey of Discovery.* (Mill Valley, CA: Nataraj Publishing, 1993; originally published by New World Library, 1989).

Gawain, Shakti. *Awakening: A Daily Guide to Conscious Living.* (Mill Valley, CA: Nataraj Publishing, 1993; originally published by New World Library, 1991).

Hendrix, Harville. *Getting the Love You Want.* (New York: Henry Holt & Co., 1988).

Luvaas, Tanha. *Notes from My Inner Child: I'm Always Here.* (Mill Valley, CA: Nataraj Publishing, 1993).

Metzger, Deena. *Writing for Your Life: A Guide and Companion to the Inner Worlds.* (San Francisco: HarperSan Francisco, 1992).

Osterberg, Rolf. *Corporate Renaissance: Business as an Adventure in Human Development.* (Mill Valley, CA: Nataraj Publishing, 1993).

Nelson, Martia. *Coming Home: The Return to True Self.* (Mill Valley, CA: Nataraj Publishing, 1993).

Roth, Gabrielle. *Maps to Ecstasy: Teachings of an Urban Shaman.* (Mill Valley, CA: Nataraj Publishing, 1993; originally published by New World Library, 1989).

Stone, Hal and Sidra. *Embracing Our Selves: The Voice Dialogue Manual.* (Mill Valley, CA: Nataraj Publishing, 1993; originally published by New World Library, 1989).

Stone, Hal and Sidra. *Embracing Each Other: Relationship as Teacher, Healer, and Guide.* (Mill Valley, CA: Nataraj Publishing, 1993; originally published by New World Library, 1989).

Stone, Hal and Sidra. *Embracing Your Inner Critic: Turning Self-Criticism into a Creative Asset.* (San Francisco: HarperSan Francisco, 1993).

Audiotapes and Videotapes:

Gawain, Shakti: TEACHING AND MEDITATION AUDIOTAPES:

> *Creative Visualization.* (San Rafael, CA: New World Library).
>
> *Developing Intuition.* (Mill Valley, CA: Nataraj Publishing).
>
> *Relationships as Mirrors.* (San Rafael, CA: New World Library).
>
> *Contacting Your Inner Guide.* (San Rafael, CA: New World Library).
>
> *The Male and Female Within.* (San Rafael, CA: New World Library).
>
> *Discovering Your Inner Child.* (San Rafael, CA: New World Library).
>
> *Expressing Your Creative Being.* (San Rafael, CA: New World Library).

Gawain, Shakti. *Living in the Light: Book on Tape.* Abridged version of the book. (Mill Valley, CA: Nataraj Publishing, 1993).

Gawain, Shakti. *The Path of Transformation: Book on Tape.* Abridged version of the book. (Mill Valley, CA: Nataraj Publishing, 1993).

Gawain, Shakti. *The Path of Transformation.* Videotape of live talk. (Carson, CA: Hay House, Inc., 1992).

Roth, Gabrielle: MUSIC AUDIOTAPES TO MOVE TO:

> *Initiation.* (New Jersey: Raven Recordings, 1988)
>
> *Bones.* (New Jersey: Raven Recordings, 1989).
>
> *Ritual.* (New Jersey: Raven Recordings, 1990).
>
> *Waves.* (New Jersey: Raven Recordings, 1991).
>
> *Trance.* (New Jersey: Raven Recordings, 1992).

Roth, Gabrielle, *Ecstatic Dance: A Workout for Body and Soul.* Movement video. (New Jersey: Raven Recordings, 1993).

Stone, Hal and Sidra: TEACHING AUDIOTAPES

> *Meeting Your Selves.* (Albion, CA: Delos)
> *The Child Within.* (Albion, CA: Delos)
> *Meet Your Inner Critic.* (Albion, CA: Delos)
> *Meet the Pusher.* (Albion, CA: Delos)
> *The Dance of Selves in Relationship.* (Albion, CA: Delos)
> *Understanding Your Relationships.* (Albion, CA: Delos)
> *Decoding Your Dreams.* (Albion, CA: Delos)
> *The Patriarch Within.* (Albion, CA: Delos, 1993)

For information about Shakti Gawain's books and tapes, and other titles published by Nataraj Publishing, New World Library, Delos, or Raven Recordings, write for a free catalog:

Nataraj Publishing
P.O. Box 2430
Mill Valley, CA 94942

To order with VISA or MasterCard, call (800) 949-1091.

Workshops:

Shakti Gawain gives talks and leads workshops all over the United States and in many other countries. She also conducts retreats, intensives, and training programs. If you would like to be on her mailing list and receive workshop information, write or call:

Shakti Gawain, Inc.
P.O. Box 377
Mill Valley, CA 94942
Telephone: (415) 388-7140

Shakti and her husband, Jim Burns, rent rooms and a guest cottage at their beautiful estate on the Hawaiian island of Kauai, for individuals and couples wishing to come for personal retreats. For information or to make reservations, call or write:

Kai Mana
P.O. Box 612
Kilauea, Hawaii 96754
Telephone: (808) 828-1280

For information about Drs. Hal and Sidra Stone's workshops and trainings, write to:

Delos
P.O. Box 604
Albion, CA 95410

For information about Gabrielle Roth's workshops, write or call:

Raven Recording
P.O. Box 2034
Red Bank, N.J. 07701
Telephone: 1-800-76-RAVEN

ABOUT THE AUTHOR

Shakti Gawain is the bestselling author of *Creative Visualization, Living in the Light, Return to the Garden, Awakening,* and several other books. A warm, articulate, and inspiring teacher, Shakti leads workshops internationally. For nearly twenty years, she has facilitated thousands of people in learning to trust and act on their own inner truth, thus releasing and developing their creativity in every area of their lives.

Shakti and her husband, Jim Burns, have recently created their own company, Nataraj Publishing. They make their home in Mill Valley, California, and on the island of Kauai.

NATARAJ PUBLISHING is committed to acting as a catalyst for change and transformation in the world by providing books and tapes on the leading edge in the fields of personal and social consciousness growth. *Nataraj* is a Sanskrit word referring to the creative, transformative power of the universe. For more information on our company, please contact us at:

Nataraj Publishing
P.O. Box 2430, Mill Valley, CA 94942
Phone: (415) 388-7195
E-mail: nataraj@nataraj.com • Website: http://www.nataraj.com

WORKSHOPS

Shakti Gawain gives talks and leads workshops all over the United States and in many other countries. She also conducts retreats, intensives, and training programs. If you would like to be on her mailing list and receive workshop information, write or call:

Shakti Gawain, Inc.
P.O. Box 377, Mill Valley, CA 94942
Telephone: (415) 388-7140

Shakti and her husband, Jim Burns, rent rooms and a guest cottage at their beautiful estate on the Hawaiian island of Kauai, for individuals and couples wishing to come for personal retreats. For information or to make reservations, call or write:

Kai Mana, P.O. Box 612, Kilauea, HI 96754
Telephone: (808) 828-1280
Fax: (808) 828-6670

BOOKS AND AUDIOCASSETTES FROM NATARAJ PUBLISHING

Books

Awakening the Warrior Within. By Dawn Callan. (Tradepaper $12.95)

Awakening: A Daily Guide to Conscious Living. By Shakti Gawain. (Tradepaper $9.95)

Coming Home: The Return to True Self. By Martia Nelson. (Tradepaper $12.95)

Corporate Renaissance: Business as an Adventure in Human Development. By Rolf Osterberg. (Hardcover $18.95)

Embracing Each Other: Relationship as Teacher, Healer, and Guide. By Drs. Hal and Sidra Stone. (Tradepaper $10.95)

Embracing Our Selves: The Voice Dialogue Manual. By Drs. Hal and Sidra Stone. (Tradepaper $12.95)

Living in the Light: A Guide to Personal and Planetary Transformation. By Shakti Gawain, with Laurel King. (Tradepaper $11.95)

Living in the Light Workbook. By Shakti Gawain. (Tradepaper $11.95)

Maps to Ecstasy: Teachings of an Urban Shaman. By Gabrielle Roth. (Tradepaper $10.95)

Notes from My Inner Child: I'm Always Here. (Tradepaper $8.95)

Passion to Heal: The Ultimate Guide to Your Healing Journey. By Echo Bodine. (Tradepaper $14.95)

The Path of Transformation: How Healing Ourselves Can Change the World. By Shakti Gawain. (Tradepaper $11.95)

Return to the Garden: A Journey of Discovery. By Shakti Gawain. (Tradepaper $11.95)

The Revelation: A Message of Hope for the New Millennium. By Barbara Marx Hubbard. (Tradepaper $16.95)

The Shadow King: The Invisible Force That Holds Women Back. By Sidra Stone, Ph.D. (Tradepaper $12.95)

The Turtle Tattoo: Timeless Tales for Finding and Fulfilling Your Dreams. By Margaret Olivia Wolfson. (Hardcover $14.95)

What Women & Men Reallly Want: Creating Deeper Understanding & Love in Our Relationships. By Aaron Kipnis, Ph.D., and Elizabeth Herron, M.A. (Tradepaper $12.95)

Write from the Heart: Unleashing the Power of Your Creativity. By Hal Zina Bennett. (Tradepaper $11.95)

Audiocassettes

Developing Intuition. Shakti Gawain. (One audiocassette $10.95)

The Four Levels of Healing. Shakti Gawain. (Two-tape set $14.95)

Living in the Light: A Guide to Personal and Planetary Transformation. Shakti Gawain. (Two-tape set $15.95)

The Path of Transformation: How Healing Ourselves Can Change the World. Shakti Gawain. (Two-tape set $15.95)

For more information on our company, please contact us at:

Nataraj Publishing
P.O. Box 2430
Mill Valley, CA 94942

To place an order, call: (800) 949-1091